LET'S KILL DICK AND JANE

LET'S KILL DICK & JANE

How the Open Court Publishing Company Fought the Culture of American Education

HAROLD HENDERSON

ST. AUGUSTINE'S PRESS
South Bend, Indiana
2006

Manufactured in the United States of America.

1 2 3 4 5 6   11 10 09 08 07 06

Library of Congress Cataloging in Publication Data
Henderson, Harold, 1948–
Let's kill Dick and Jane: how the Open Court Publishing Company fought the culture of American education / Harold Henderson.
p.   cm.
ISBN 1-58731-919-5 (hardcover: alk. paper)
1. Textbooks – United States. 2. Textbooks – Publishing – Social aspects – United States. 3. Open Court Publishing Company – History. 4. Educational change – United States. 5. Educational publishing – United States. I. Title.
LB3047.H46 2006
371.3'2 – dc22   2006010140

∞ The paper used in this publication meets the minimum requirements of the American National Standard for Information Sciences – Permanence of Paper for Printed Materials, ANSI Z39.48-1984.

St. Augustine's Press
www.staugustine.net

Contents

Acknowledgments

This book would not exist if André Carus had not persuaded me to write it as a cultural study rather than a corporate history. The financial arrangement was simple: I took one-quarter time off my job as staff writer for the *Chicago Reader*, and he paid me the difference as an independent contractor. Neither he nor anyone else with the company told me what to write. Had they done so, I could have gone back to full-time work at the *Reader* at any time, and would have done so. Any mistakes or losses of perspective are mine alone. Special thanks to Rose Piltaver for guiding me through the Open Court archives and to all those who took the time to answer my questions. Quotations not from the readily available published literature are from the Open Court archives.

Introduction

> *"Education is the acquisition of the art of the utilisation of knowledge. This is an art very difficult to impart. Whenever a text-book is written of real educational worth, you may be quite certain that some reviewer will say that it will be difficult to teach from it. Of course it will be difficult to teach from it. If it were easy, the book ought to be burned; for it cannot be educational."* – Alfred North Whitehead, *The Aims of Education*

This book draws on the history of one small textbook publisher to argue that we need to think differently about education. In particular, we need to distance ourselves from the two grossly stereotyped "sides" that most of us almost automatically fall into when we talk about schools.

"Traditionalists" in education value order, intellect, and excellence. They want children to master a definite body of knowledge. Therefore they believe everyone should study pretty much the same things. To accomplish this goal, they favor lectures, drill, reading, and testing. The teacher is seen as an authority whose main job is to teach students what he or she knows and they don't. They gravitate toward movements like phonics in beginning reading and back-to-basics in math.

"Progressives" in education value freedom, self-expression, and equity. They want children to enjoy learning and learn what they enjoy. Therefore they believe the curriculum should be tailored to individual needs and wants. To accomplish this goal, they favor discussion, informal play or games, multimedia, and evaluation (if any) by portfolio or other nonstandard means. Teachers are seen as friends or facilitators who help students discover new knowledge for themselves. They gravitate toward movements like look-say or whole language in reading and constructivist math.

1

These two polar viewpoints are all too familiar. Unfortunately, they don't reflect reality, and they don't help us think clearly about what goes on in school, for at least two reasons.

The first reason is just common sense: each side has a firm grip on only part of the truth. At the simplest level, most people would take a "traditional" attitude toward the education of medical students, but a "progressive" view of how to introduce first-graders to painting. "At their best," writes Diane Ravitch in *Left Back: A Century of Failed School Reforms,* "both philosophies have made valuable and complementary contributions to American education. Progressive educators can justly take credit for emphasizing students' motivation and understanding and making the schools responsible for the health and general welfare of children. Traditionalists such as Harris, Bagley, and Hirsch must be credited for insisting upon the democratic responsibility of the school to promote the intellectual growth of all children. At their best, these traditions overlap and the differences between them become blurred because thoughtful educators, regardless of label, seek to develop their students' intellect and character."

The second reason to take neither side is less familiar and perhaps more controversial. Neither traditionalism nor progressivism has much to do with day-to-day classroom practice. This book argues that American public education is dominated by a culture that resists both ideologies, a culture that maintains a status quo that is mediocre by either standard. Even if one side were to win the public intellectual battle waged in professional journals and conference speeches and commission reports, its victory would have little effect on culturally supported classroom routines that both sides deplore.

The American education culture often takes a high-sounding educational goal from either side, translates it into a series of activities, and then pursues those activities for their own sake. On the traditional side, the goal of understanding literature is translated into the routine of answering the comprehension questions printed after each story in the reader. Teachers come to think that their students can't learn to understand literature without such questions. On the progressive side, "appreciate scientific method" becomes "complete a 'science project,'" and nothing else will do because "science projects" have become an institution.

Traditionalists and progressives alike will shudder and say, "That's not what we meant." Of course it isn't. But that's what the culture does to their big ideas. What should be means become ends in themselves, while the ends are neglected. The students may never even hear of them. At the level of everyday schooling, it makes little sense to argue progressive versus traditional. The problem is the education culture. It is neither, and it can turn schools into thought-free zones.

*   *   *   *   *

Open Court Publishing Company grew out of traditionalism and often publicly identified with it. But from the beginning, the company's textbooks blended traditionalist and progressive approaches. "Open Court is child-centered in the sense that we are encouraging children to take on more responsibility," founder Blouke Carus told the superintendent of the Cincinnati Public Schools in 1987, "but this cannot be done by abdicating classroom authority or abandoning structure."

From its founding in 1962 through its sale in 1996, this small Midwestern publisher challenged the education culture. Recognizing that textbooks determine what is taught in most classrooms most of the time, it sought to enable all students, rather than just a small elite, to think on their own. You can't get much more traditional, much more progressive – or much more ambitious – than that. "No one knows whether it can be done," wrote Ravitch in *The American Scholar* in 1984, "because we have never tried to do it on a mass scale."

Why not? According to Ravitch, "The perfervid traditionalists have been content to educate those at the top without regard to the welfare of the majority of students," while "the perfervid progressives have cooperated in dividing and diluting the curriculum, which left the majority with an inadequate education." Meanwhile the muddled majority in between remains enmeshed in the interlocking, self-reinforcing system of practices, ideas, and attitudes that make up the dominant culture of American public education.

This culture is pervasive, and yet it's hard for would-be reformers to see or name. In a commentary published at EducationNews.org in January 2001, conservative Jann Flury complained, "The education bureaucracy has a life of its own. It refuses to listen or bow to sage advice, and it will not accept ideas to improve student learning. This pedagogical entity has turned into a huge amorphous blob not unlike a monstrous, growing mound of dough. It pervades everything as it gains in mass." Progressive-minded educational historian Larry Cuban, in *How Teachers Taught,* was disconcerted to find how much the classrooms he visited in the 1980s looked and felt like the ones he inhabited during the 1940s. And in the 1970s, the incomparable education polemicist Richard Mitchell wrote in *Less Than Words Can Say,* "The problem isn't here and it isn't there; it's everywhere. If we want to do only so simple a thing as ensure that all third-grade teachers will be expert in spelling and punctuation, we will have to change everything that happens at every step of the process by which we now provide ourselves with third-grade teachers."

The education culture is the background against which overt, newsworthy disagreements over transportation, teachers, and textbooks are played out. It's taken for granted in the same way that most people take for granted family Thanksgiving dinner. No one familiar with American culture expects to peruse a printed menu before such a dinner, or to leave a tip afterwards. No one but an anthropologist even imagines such a possibility. Like Thanksgiving dinner, the education culture's ways are learned mainly from experience, not from books. And, like Thanksgiving dinner, those who challenge its ways are often misunderstood, or ignored as some kind of absurd embarrassment.

In substance, the American education culture is anti-intellectual. In form, it's interconnected and self-repairing. James Stigler and James Hiebert offer a simple example in their book *The Teaching Gap.* The American cultural assumption is that teaching math consists primarily of teaching students to perform procedures, such as multiplying two-digit numbers. Understanding how and why a given procedure works is secondary at best. Accordingly, many teachers use overhead projectors to focus students' attention on each step as the teacher demonstrates it. In Japan, the cultural assumption is quite different. There, teaching math is believed to consist primarily of teaching students to understand the relations between facts, principles, and ideas. Accordingly teachers there use the chalkboard to record an entire lesson, leaving it all visible so that students can refer back and confirm their understanding.

Stigler and Hiebert point out that simply mandating use of the chalkboard instead of the overhead projector in American schools would not provoke deeper reform, nor would it change American teachers' implicit view of mathematics. "If all teachers in the United States started using the chalkboard rather than the overhead projector, teaching would not change much. The chalkboard simply would be used to fill the visual-aids slot in their system and therefore would be used just as the overhead projector was – to catch and hold students' attention."

Ancient alchemists sought to change lead into gold. As the above hypothetical example suggests, the education culture does the opposite. It has an uncanny ability to transform golden ideas for change – from left, right, or center – into a leaden sludge. The history of Open Court textbooks confirms how difficult it is for reforms that sound good on the 10 PM news to reach the 9 AM class in recognizable form. Even seemingly clear-cut, small-scale innovations – far more specific than those usually proposed in legislation or commission reports – are defanged in this way. For instance, acting on sound pedagogical principle, Open Court always refused to develop a separate spelling program disconnected from learning to read, write, listen, and speak. (The company had a strategy for teaching kids to spell, but it didn't involve a separate book or rote lists.) Teachers using Open Court textbooks were nevertheless frequently found to be creating traditional "spelling lists" on their own for students to memorize and be tested on. Research, theory, explanation, and encouragement did not deter them.

It would completely miss the point to blame the teachers alone. No one group controls the culture, and no one group can change it. Arbitrary lists of spelling words were expected by students, parents, and supervisors – everyone involved in school. Without lists, it seemed as if "the kids aren't being taught to spell." The culture is interlocking.

A more drastic example of the culture's power – and its imperviousness to ideological labels – comes from the spring and summer of 1984, when Open Court salespeople reconnoitered the state of Florida in order to decide whether the company should make a major effort in the state to sell its thinking-oriented *Real Math* textbooks for grades 1 through 6.

On paper, Florida looked like a promising market. The state's official "Standards of Excellence" favored Open Court's emphasis on problem solving and reasoning over drill. But the standards were a dead letter, because the state judged teachers and schools only on students' ability to perform simple, isolated mathematical calculations. Nor did this seem to bother the teachers. Math supervisors knew that their students were having trouble with decimals, fractions, division, money, and word problems – but they did not wonder why the kids were struggling. They thought they knew, and according to Open Court's Jan Holland, they asked for "an instant cure in the form of *more* diagnostic tests, *more* skill sheets, and *more* tests to measure objectives."

The math supervisors talked a good game. Using the words of the National Council of Teachers of Mathematics and *Real Math,* they said they wanted to teach problem solving. But they meant teaching students "to look for *key words* in solving word problems" – teaching them, for instance, to spot the word "left" in a word problem and proceed at once to subtract the smaller number from the larger! If that wasn't enough to discourage dissidents, Nick Vigilante of Florida International University, who taught teachers in summer math institutes, advised teachers, "You can't teach problem solving. You either have it or you don't."

Holland was appalled to find that "many primary teachers do not even *read* to their children." At one school in St. Lucie

County, the teachers "couldn't believe all the reading they had to do with the *primary* Thinking Stories [in the *Real Math* books] and asked if we didn't have these on tape." In despair, Holland concluded, "We're trying to teach children to think when the teachers don't want to think."

If anything is going to change, this culture must change. Like most school reformers, Blouke Carus started Open Court's textbook program in the expectation that upgrading one element would improve all the rest. When this didn't happen, he found himself face to face with the education culture. (He recalls forming what he called Carus's Law: "Every good idea in education sooner or later gets perverted.") This book tells the rest of the story. It offers no magic formula for changing the culture. First we must render it visible.

*   *   *   *   *

Open Court reading and math textbooks were used with success in hundreds of thousands of classrooms during its 34 years of existence as a separate company. But they were not used in millions more.

When a reform idea or an improved product fails to catch on, sooner or later someone must ask why. If your mousetrap was really so much better, why didn't it sell? Was there something wrong with the product? Was there something wrong with the people making, selling, and managing it? Was there not enough money? Or was there something wrong with the (potential) customers?

The correct answer in Open Court's case is surely "all of the above." Open Court's textbooks and related materials could have been better and easier to use than they were. The company's management was often lacking, whether it was in the hands of family members and old-timers who understood its educational vision, or of newcomers who understood good business and management practices. The company's finances were shaky or worse.

As for the customers, Open Court had been founded on the belief that there *was* something wrong with its potential customers – in other words, that schools need to change. Open

Court was trying to change the market it sold in, by selling better products. It was simultaneously an education-reform organization and a business.

Because it was reformist, Open Court confronted the American education culture from day one. Because it was a business, it could not retreat from that confrontation into bombast or ivory-tower theorizing. Its need to survive as a business meant that Open Court's *reform* efforts probably had more impact on classrooms – actually helping students to read and think – than did most products of the post-Sputnik curriculum-reform era.

The tension between business and reform did not just divide Open Court from the education culture. It also divided the company itself, at every level. Some members of the Carus family, which owned it, were unenthusiastic about the business potential of Blouke's reformism. Within the company's ranks, those who sold the books (who were most in touch with the culture of education) often saw things differently from those who put them together (who were most in touch with the intellectuals who wanted to change the schools).

A full corporate history of Open Court would be longer than this book. It would go into detail about the company's internal power struggles, management failures, financial crises, and programs hastily put together at the last minute. This book mentions some of these episodes but doesn't dwell on them. They're important if you want to figure out all the reasons why this particular small company failed to sustain itself economically and was sold in 1996. (McGraw-Hill's subsequent success with the program is a very relevant sequel to this story, but a different story nonetheless.) But these episodes are of less interest if you want to know what Open Court's 34 years of selling reform can tell us about the education culture. How is it verbalized and acted out? How does it maintain itself under siege? How has it adapted over the years? Why has it been so successful in resisting reform?

1. What is the problem? (1900–1962)

"A major sin of modern education, in all branches of the curriculum, has been the unwillingness to demand serious effort." – Douglas Bush, in *The Case for Basic Education*, 1959

NO GOLDEN AGE

IN 1959, ANDRÉ Carus started first grade twice – that spring in the German town of Gummersbach, and again that fall in La Salle, Illinois. His parents, Blouke and Marianne, got an unexpected education themselves in the process. "His [German] reader was only half an inch thick," Blouke recalled later, "yet at the end of first grade it was challenging. . . . Each story had real characters; the selections were real stories or poems."

Back in the United States, the Caruses were horrified to find that his textbooks contained almost no text! "I can still see us looking at them," recalls Marianne Carus. "His science book had a great big picture of the sun and underneath it one word: 'SUN.' I think we threw them out."

Many critics in recent years had pointed out the inadequacy of American education, among them Mortimer Smith (*And Madly Teach,* 1949), Arthur Bestor (*Educational Wastelands,* 1953), and Rudolf Flesch (*Why Johnny Can't Read,* 1955). The Caruses did not have to read these books to know there was a problem. Unlike most American parents, they had seen it with their own eyes.

But what exactly was the problem? Was it just that American textbooks were dumb and German textbooks intelligent? Or was it that American textbooks had been intelligent once – the nineteenth-century McGuffey Readers, perhaps – and had since been dumbed down?

Many critics believed that all students had once learned to

read, write, figure, and understand history, science, and art. For instance, Mortimer Smith lamented in the September 1961 "Bulletin" of the Council for Basic Education that in 1910 some 83 percent of high-schoolers had been enrolled in a foreign language class, and only 21 percent in 1955.

This image of a lost Golden Age in American education helped fuel a movement to make schools more academically demanding. But as a picture of the world it is so incomplete as to be false. At the turn of the century, when American schools focused on traditional academic pursuits, they educated only a minority of American children. Smith's percentages are accurate but misleading. In 1910, the 83 percent taking foreign languages were roughly 1 million of the 1.2 million students enrolled in high school. In 1955, there were 6.9 million high-schoolers, and as Smith said, only 21 percent of them were taking a foreign language – but 21 percent of 6.9 million is 1.4 million, *more* students than in 1910! The numbers describe a less than ideal situation, but they do not tell a simple story of decline and fall.

There was no Golden Age. How could there be, when only 20 percent of the American soldiers who fought in World War I had finished eighth grade? A quarter-century later, in World War II, that figure had risen to almost 70 percent. No wonder American schools and textbooks changed. For the first time they had to teach the children of all socio-economic classes for more than a few months. To do so, they followed the path of least resistance in a nation that had never been friendly to intellectual endeavor – and made a virtue of this makeshift.

American schools have not deteriorated – they've never been good enough. As literacy authorities Lawrence Stedman and Carl Kaestle put it in *Literacy in the United States: Readers and Reading since 1880,* "Even if schools today are performing about as well as they have in the past, they have never excelled at educating minorities and the poor or at teaching higher-order skills."

The admirable Clifton Fadiman used to sigh that all children had once learned to read without so much fuss about the correct teaching method. He too missed the demographic point: when you try to teach reading to large numbers of children whose families pay little attention to written language, the difficulty of the task becomes obvious in a way that it was not before.

"The traditional methods of teaching reading and arithmetic were not abandoned without reason," explained Open Court author Carl Bereiter some years later. "The job of reconstruction, as for instance in Open Court's reading and mathematics programs, has not been merely to recover the good but to devise ways of making the good work under contemporary conditions, with the kind of pupils – and teachers – who currently exist."

American education cannot improve by returning to the 1890s. Nevertheless the Golden Age idea got a movement started. Over time the Caruses, along with a few others, went beyond it. They began to articulate an unprecedented and more radical question, one that did not depend on misreading the past: How can we educate our masses as rigorously as Europeans do their elite? This book is about their efforts to answer this question in practice – and their difficulty in finding educators at any level who were willing even to ask it.

CARUS ROOTS

Open Court Publishing Company would never have published its textbooks, let alone asked such a question, if the Carus family had not had roots in both Europe and North America. In 1856 young engineer Edward Hegeler – Blouke Carus's great-grandfather – and his partner Frederick Matthiessen emigrated from Germany. They established a zinc factory in La Salle, Illinois, which prospered and made them both rich. In 1887, Hegeler founded Open Court Publishing Company for "the transplanting of European (especially German) thought to America."

Paul Carus, a more recent immigrant from Germany and Blouke Carus's grandfather, soon joined the Open Court enterprise and married Hegeler's daughter Mary. Under his direction Open Court published hundreds of philosophical books and two regular magazines (*The Open Court* and *The Monist*). A networker long before the word was coined, Paul Carus published and conducted dialogues with such leading thinkers as Charles Peirce, William James, D.T. Suzuki, and Ernst Mach. After his death in

1919, his widow Mary and daughter Elisabeth maintained the publishing operation on a reduced scale under the auspices of the family's Hegeler Foundation.

Paul and Mary's oldest son Edward, a mathematician, founded Carus Chemical Company in 1915 and fathered five children, including Blouke. When the family visited Germany in 1939, twelve-year-old Blouke got a brief but never-forgotten taste of German liberal-arts education. He attended *Gymnasium* in Freiburg from Easter until the end of July. Its seriousness made a bigger impression on him than its exclusivity. (At that time, less than 10 percent of German students attended *Gymnasium*.) "I wondered, 'Why are these kids working so hard?' Back in La Salle, you were odd if you studied hard."

Blouke chose to attend Cal Tech, not just for its engineering training but because of its humanities requirements. After graduating in 1949, he revisited Europe. In Freiburg once again, he studied chemistry and met and married Marianne Sondermann, a match that strengthened the family's European ties. They moved to La Salle in 1951 and started a family; Blouke went to work at Carus Chemical Company. He began searching for a more efficient way to produce the company's main product, the oxidant potassium permanganate.

Photographs reveal a dark-haired young man, slim, almost wispy in stature. A somewhat bland exterior concealed the intensity with which he pursued the new permanganate process. Persevering against the conventional wisdom, he eventually succeeded, providing a steady source of revenue for the company. The experience gained him several patents, plus self-confidence and a set of skills that proved useful later on. Among these skills he identifies a willingness to change course when faced with new facts. "You had to eliminate any ego involvement. If there was anything better available from any source, you'd better apply it or you'd be left behind." In contrast, as he was soon to learn, "The education professors would get stuck on one or two ideas and never deviated from them."

An engineer by training, a problem-solver by temperament, and a Midwesterner by birth and upbringing, Blouke was neither a highbrow nor a rebel, although his makeup included elements of both. Recreations he and Marianne enjoyed in the 1950s in La Salle included Great Books discussion groups and chamber music. He was well enough educated to appreciate the Western cultural tradition – and to appreciate that he did not know it as well as his forebears had.

"My own education has been woefully inadequate," he said later. "In a very real sense, in school I was deprived of my literary and cultural heritage and my training in writing was a farce." The idea that he could help others become acquainted with that heritage was to prove immensely appealing to him. But he might never have formulated or acted on it if the schools had been more open in the first place.

2. What should children do in school?

"Are schools too resistant to change or too faddish? Viewed over the course of history, they may seem to be both. Educators have often paid lip service to demands for reform to signify their alertness to the public will. But their symbolic responses often protected school people from basic challenges to their core practices." – David Tyack and Larry Cuban, *Tinkering Toward Utopia: A Century of Public School Reform*, 1995

FROM THE ACADEMIC TO THE USEFUL

DURING THE EARLY 1900s, an unprecedented number of American children came to school and stayed longer – just as American educators were disagreeing more than ever about what they should be doing there. The great increase in numbers all but required change. No longer was it assumed that students should discipline their intellects by learning the same traditional subjects in the same traditional ways as earlier generations had. The question, as historian Richard Hofstadter puts it in *Anti-Intellectualism in American Life*, was how the schools should change: "whether the academic content and intellectual standards of the school should be made as high as possible for each child, according to his will and his capacities, or whether there was good ground for abandoning any such end."

This choice was not so much made as it was pre-empted. "The problem of numbers had hardly made its appearance before a movement began in professional education to exalt numbers over quality and the alleged demands of utility over intellectual development," writes Hofstadter. Educators "were not content to say that the realities of American social life had made it necessary to compromise with the ideal of education as the development of formal learning and intellectual capacity. Instead, they militantly

14

proclaimed that such education was archaic and futile and that the noblest end of a truly democratic system of education was to meet the child's immediate interests by offering him a series of immediate utilities."

The only remaining issue, as described in Herbert Kliebard's *The Struggle for the American Curriculum 1893–1958,* was which immediate utilities would take precedence. Should students follow their natural developmental tendencies and interests? Should they learn what they needed in order to do their future jobs, enumerated in precise factory-style lists of curriculum objectives? Should they learn what they needed to reconstruct society along more humane lines? Or should they study life-adjustment topics like "personality, etiquette, family living and vocations"?

Educators ultimately said "yes" in different ways to each of these divergent notions, sometimes incongruously bundled together and labeled "progressive education." Every approach – the academic, the child-centered, the vocational, the reconstructionist, the life-adjustment – managed to leave its imprint on the schools without obliterating the others. Thus it was possible to have schools, organized in part according to the same old subjects, where teachers espoused child-centered practices and sometimes reformist politics, while supervisors managed according to efficiency experts' studies of factory work. Advocates of any one approach could claim victory, or victimhood, just by focusing on a particular part of the system.

FROM THE CHILD-CENTERED CURRICULUM TO "NOT EVERYONE NEEDS TO READ"

Even a truly child-centered curriculum, which is what many people mean when they say "progressive education," could have been demanding. In the 1890s John Dewey worried that children were cut off from useful involvement in daily life. He proposed that schools should postpone academic subjects in favor of real-life experiences.

Such a curriculum might well have asked more of teachers than the repetitive drills of the previous era ever had. "The demand on the teacher is twofold," explains historian Lawrence

Cremin in *The Transformation of the School: Progressivism in American Education 1876–1957*: "thorough knowledge of the disciplines and an awareness of those common experiences of childhood that can be utilized to lead children toward . . . this knowledge." In other words, "to recognize opportunities for early mathematical learning, one must know mathematics; to recognize opportunities for elementary scientific learning, one must know physics, chemistry, biology, and geology; and so on down the list of fields of knowledge." By this reasoning, the ideal child-centered teacher should be a well-educated and quick-witted liberal-arts major indeed.

It's hard to see how this could have happened, even if anyone had made such a breathtaking suggestion. American schools employed more than twice as many classroom teachers in 1940 (875,000) as in 1900 (423,000). James Koerner deplored what he considered the retreat of liberal-arts scholars from American education, and shuddered at their replacement by "the 'professional' educator, a relatively new kind of schoolman who, specializing in pedagogical and administrative technique, has grown to astonishing numbers in a short time." But Koerner did not explain where an extra half-million scholars were to be found on short notice in a country where scholarship had always been a marginal pursuit.

Thus it was that when Marianne Carus first began helping out in the Open Court textbook office in the early 1960s, she was appalled at the number of spelling mistakes she found in teachers' letters to the company. "I thought they were supposed to be a model for students." She was accustomed to Germany, where teachers in the *Gymnasium* were members of the national cultural elite. In the U.S., by contrast, there was no institutionalized cultural elite. Demography among other factors had spawned an education culture that was fundamentally anti-intellectual, as abundantly documented by Diane Ravitch in *Left Back: A Century of Failed School Reforms*.

By the time Marianne started slitting envelopes, those new teaching posts had been filled by tens of thousands who had studied under William Heard Kilpatrick of Columbia Teachers College and his ilk. In the 1920s Kilpatrick and others went Dewey one better, popularizing the notion that the world was changing so fast that it made no sense to teach subject matter fixed in advance. They attacked the "cold storage" view of knowledge, in which facts and skills were stored up for future use. They sought to deemphasize the acquisition of knowledge in favor of "purposeful activity."

Kilpatrick's views had the effect of discrediting subject matter and making it easy for teachers to substitute child-centeredness *tout court* for a child-centered curriculum. The purposeful activity he prescribed soon devolved into activity for its own sake, as life-adjustment education began to permeate the schools in the 1940s. A U.S. Office of Education conference in 1945 resolved unanimously that schools should prepare 20 percent of their students for college, train another 20 percent for "desirable skilled occupations," and give the remaining 60 percent "the life-adjustment training they need." A contemporary teacher trainer identified the goals of education as "the development of physical health, mental and emotional stability, fine personality and effective citizenship."

A.H. Lauchner, principal of Thornburn Junior High School in Urbana, Illinois, spelled out the implications for earlier grades. "Not every child has to read, figure, write and spell," he wrote in the March 1951 issue of the *Bulletin of the National Association of Secondary-School Principals,* an obscure publication made infamous by Arthur Bestor's quoting from it. "If and when we are able to convince a few folks that mastery of reading, writing, and arithmetic is not the one road leading to happy, successful living, the next step is to cut down the amount of time and attention devoted to these areas in general junior high-school courses." This is not a parody, although it may read like one at this distance in time. Lauchner's views were altogether typical. In the years that followed this publication, he moved up in his profession, becoming a school principal in Great Neck, New York, and holding a visiting faculty appointment at Northwestern University's School of Education.

THE 1950S CRITICS

Universal public education, once seen as a victory for democracy, had somehow led American educators to consign most of their students to dead-end courses in life adjustment. This paradox gave an opening to the advocates of academic-centered education. They argued that their seemingly elitist approach would prove more democratic in the long run.

As a result, the 1950s were anything but quiet. Even before the Soviets created a panic by launching Sputnik on October 4, 1957, the decade was "a period of criticism of American education unequaled in modern times," according to Herbert Kliebard. Critics like Mortimer Smith and Arthur Bestor fired rhetorical salvos at the barn-sized target offered by life-adjustment education. "It enthrones once again the ancient doctrine," Bestor wrote in 1953, "that a clear majority of the people are destined from birth to be hewers of wood and drawers of water for a select and superior few."

Bestor's critique of the whole public-school curriculum in *Educational Wastelands* and *The Restoration of Learning* never caught on in the way that a more narrowly focused book did in 1955. Rudolf Flesch's *Why Johnny Can't Read* spent thirty-nine weeks on the best-seller list, and its title has entered the language. Flesch excoriated school professionals for teaching children to read by the "look-say" method. "The teaching of reading – all over the United States, in all the schools, in all the textbooks – is totally wrong and flies in the face of all logic and common sense," he wrote. In fact, "Johnny's only problem [is] that he was unfortunately exposed to an ordinary American school."

Flesch attacked the teaching of reading, but he did not join in the broader critique of schools. He endorsed child-centered progressive education, agreeing that schooling should be "democratic, free of senseless formalism and drill, based on interest and meaningful experience, and inseparably joined to the real life that goes on around the child."

In theory, any method of teaching reading – phonics or look-say or some variation – could coexist with any philosophy of education. But in practice, contrary to Flesch's own inclinations and for reasons that remain obscure, phonics soon became associated with the traditional academic curriculum and political conservatism, look-say with the progressive child-centered curriculum and political liberalism.

Flesch viewed look-say much as the other critics viewed the overall state of American education – elitism masquerading as democracy. The schools taught reading so ineffectively, he contended, that those children who did learn how to read were likely to do so on their own or at home, with devastating implications for the American dream of social mobility.

"The child who comes from an educated, book-reading home has a tremendous advantage. The son of illiterate parents will stumble for three years through the twelve hundred words [of reading vocabulary] without help or guidance and then, as likely as not, develop into a 'non-reader.' . . . I say, therefore, that the word method is gradually destroying democracy in this country; it returns to the upper middle class the privileges that public education was supposed to distribute evenly among the people." Whether they meant to or not, at the tactical moment of the 1950s, Flesch and Bestor and Smith were concentrating their fire on the same target.

"WE HAVE NEVER REALLY TRIED TO GIVE A SERIOUS EDUCATION TO ALL STUDENTS"

As Blouke and Marianne's family grew, they began to take an interest in their local schools. In the mid-1950s Blouke joined the local Parent-Teacher Association and became its president. In 1956 he ran for the high-school board of education. He lost, but not because he espoused any unorthodox opinions. At that point he was still just asking questions.

Following his defeat, Blouke continued to question, but he did not take up with either strand of education critics. Instead he espoused a mild proposal put forth by agricultural educator Herbert McNee Hamlin of the University of Illinois. Hamlin was urging school boards to organize committees of lay people to advise and recommend policies to them. These tame groups were intended to head off independent citizens' groups which, he felt, might not represent the community and might not work "with and through the constituted school authorities."

Blouke read Hamlin's writings – *Citizens' Committees in the Public Schools* (1952) and the pamphlet "A Charter for a School-Sponsored System of Citizens' Committees" (1953) – and visited him in Champaign-Urbana. Citizens' committees promised to be a step beyond the PTA, which steered clear of curriculum matters altogether. He invited Hamlin to speak to a gathering of school superintendents and board members in the La Salle area. The local worthies heard Hamlin out but wanted no part of his proposal. As Blouke recalls, they were not just dismissive, they were "apoplectic" at any criticism.

Hamlin may have been less abrasive than Flesch or Bestor, but even his plan was not deferential enough to appeal to the administrators. They felt no need to discuss goals and policies with the community. Scientific management had been an ideal in American public schools for decades, and they were the scientific managers. Pupil numbers had skyrocketed on their watch. Credentials and teaching had become increasingly standardized (without necessarily gaining in intellectual substance) even as teachers' numbers multiplied.

When Blouke saw Hamlin's modest proposal rejected out of hand, it began to dawn on him that education was a closed system. If he wanted to do anything substantive about it, he would have to work as an outsider. He joined the fledgling Council for Basic Education, which Bestor, Smith, and others had founded in 1956.

CBE opposed the life-adjustment curriculum in particular and child-centered progressivism in general. Philosophically, it did not hold with Dewey's preference for experience over intellect. "The purpose of education . . . can be achieved only by making intellectual values central rather than peripheral in education." On a practical level and again contrary to Dewey and Kilpatrick, CBE held that children needed intellectual and cultural constants more than ever, in order to orient themselves in a world of unprecedented change. Schools should "transmit the facts about the heritage and culture of the race" and cultivate an "atmosphere of moral affirmation without which education is merely animal training." (On an even more practical level, as the U.S. competed with the Soviet Union in the Cold War, child-centered education began to look dangerously self-indulgent.)

European schools' more rigorous course of study appealed to CBE, but the group did not endorse their continuing elitism. Thus CBE's implicit goal was radical, if not always recognized as such: to give to the mass of students what half a century earlier had been available (at most) to the minority who went beyond the early grades.

Could American students handle it? "We have never really tried to give a serious education to all students," wrote James Koerner in his foreword to *The Case for Basic Education,* published in 1959 and read by Blouke soon thereafter. "Public schoolmen, far from having the answer to this most fundamental of educational problems, appear not even to have asked the question."

WHAT IVAN KNOWS THAT JOHNNY DOESN'T

Blouke shared with CBE a sense that bad ideas – specifically John Dewey's – had dragged American education down from its Golden Age glories. Blouke also had a personal reason to think so. Reading his grandfather's philosophical works in the 1950s, he had come across Paul Carus's 1908 stricture on William James, the guiding spirit of American pragmatism and one of Dewey's mentors. "With all due respect for Professor James," wrote Paul, "I would deem it a misfortune if his philosophy would ever exercise a determining and permanent influence upon the national life of our country."

Blouke's engineering background set him apart from the founders of CBE, most of whom had been educated in the humanities. CBE leaders wrote books and articles criticizing the schools. They were unlikely to undertake a personal mission to set them right. Blouke saw schooling as a problem to be solved, and business as a plausible way to solve it. He read Alfred North Whitehead's *The Aims of Education* and James Koerner's *The Case for Basic Education.* He sought out and quizzed twelve of the eighteen contributors to the latter book. "He was never afraid to approach anyone," says Marianne. He discussed teacher training with Harvard professor Harold Martin in 1959. Closer to hand, he talked with Priscilla McQueen, a childhood friend of his sister

Mary Louise. McQueen had taught aphasic children under Mildred McGinnis at the Central Institute for the Deaf in St. Louis, and was now tutoring children in the nearby small town of Tiskilwa. Most of them were not aphasic, she told Blouke. Their speech was normal. Their use and understanding of language was not impaired. But they weren't learning to read in school, and she had found that McGinnis's methods helped.

These conversations were informative, but they didn't answer the question Blouke kept asking: "How could I, with extremely limited experience in education [not to mention no resources, no leverage, and no network] ever hope to make basic improvements?" The answer came "like a thunderbolt out of the sky" during an enforced period of calm. In January 1962 a persistent stomach complaint sent him to the University of Chicago Hospital, where Marianne brought him a new book, *What Ivan Knows that Johnny Doesn't*. In it Arther Trace Jr., a professor at John Carroll University near Cleveland, argued that the Soviets were not merely ahead of the U.S. in science and technology (by then a post-Sputnik commonplace) – they were doing a better job of teaching the humanities as well.

Most American first-graders at the time were reading repetitive stories about the daily activities of Dick and Jane, stories with little ethical or literary merit. By contrast, in the Soviets' first-grade *Rodnaya Rech* reader, Trace found "2 anecdotes, 3 stories, one fable, and one fairy tale (a version of 'The Three Bears') by Leo Tolstoy; there are 3 poems by Pushkin, one fable by Krylov, a poem by Nicholas Nekrassov and one by Lermontov. There are also a rather large number of anonymous tales, poems, stories, and particularly animal fables drawn from a rich Russian folklore tradition, and which have a distinct literary value. There are also a number of selections by well-known contemporary Soviet authors. Altogether, about one-third of the selections in the first-grade *Rodnaya Rech* reader have genuine literary merit, and some are written by Russia's greatest authors."

Vocabulary levels also differed dramatically between the two countries. By fourth grade, Russian students' reading vocabulary was closing in on 10,000 words, while their American counterparts had been exposed to fewer than 1800 words in their school reading. In his later book *Reading without Dick and Jane* Trace documented the astonishingly restrictive vocabularies used in that kind of enormously popular reader series. Typical is the following note to the teacher note in the 1952 edition of the basal reader for the first half of second grade:

"The new *Friends and Neighbors* has a total vocabulary of 564 words. Of these, 229 words are new at this level; 177 were introduced at Book One level; 100 were new in the Primer; and the remaining 58 were introduced at Pre-Primer level. Each of the 564 words is used a minimum of ten times in the new *Friends and Neighbors*. No page introduces more than two of the 229 new words, and no new words are introduced in the first unit of the book. The first five uses of each of the 229 new words are bunched for easy mastery, with no gap of more than five pages between any two of these first five uses."

It seemed a safe bet to Blouke that no literature worth reading could be written to such specifications. And it laid a flimsy foundation, as Trace observed: "In the typical Dick-and-Jane type *sixth* grade readers [the written vocabulary] is less than half the [spoken] recognition vocabulary of the typical kindergartner." In other words, if children experienced reading only in school, they might reasonably conclude that it was a clumsy and inefficient substitute for talking and listening. No wonder Trace later excoriated the Dick-and-Jane type of readers as "programmed retardation."

"American schools have not, of course, abandoned the basic subjects entirely," Trace concluded in *What Ivan Knows*: "all our students do study their own language, though they don't learn it very well; they all do study literature, though not very much or very good literature; they all do study history and geography, though not very much for very long; they all do study mathematics, though many never get beyond arithmetic; most of them study a basic science, though for only a year; and some of them study a foreign language, but not long enough to learn it."

This was the episode of André's first-grade textbooks writ large, impressively documented and wittily told. However, like

Western observers of other Soviet industries, Trace may have taken too much at face value, assuming that good textbooks were used intelligently, and that serious, informed teaching was the norm in Soviet elementary classrooms. Trace also joined in the Golden Age fallacy when he wrote, "There has been a serious deterioration in the past thirty years in the intellectual content of the curriculum and textbooks of our public and parochial schools." He listed the authors anthologized in McGuffey's sixth-grade reader to show "how literary an American sixth-grade reader can be," without acknowledging the enormous difference in who was being educated in 1961 compared to 1891. Like CBE, Trace was in fact proposing not a return to the past, but a leap into an untried future.

"ALL THAT IS NEEDED IS A LITTLE DETERMINATION"

Whatever its long-range implications, in January 1962 Trace's book gave Blouke just what he needed. It showed him where to put his lever so as to move the educational planet, and convinced him that it could be moved. American schools, Trace contended, could improve their offerings in literature and history without spending more money, because "a good textbook does not cost any more than a bad textbook." Trace said he couldn't find any good textbooks – no surprise given the absence of economic incentive he described! Nevertheless, he asserted that his proposals could be carried out cheaply. "All that is needed is a little determination and hard work."

Blouke emerged from the hospital with his stomach trouble undiagnosed but a healthy newborn idea instead: school improvement through textbook reform. Open Court had long published philosophical books. Blouke soon persuaded other family members – his father, the trustee of the family foundation, in particular – that the company could provide a "profound and lasting service" by branching out into elementary textbooks providing a quality alternative to the near-monopoly of Dick-and-Jane style readers – thus "doing something about the Achilles heel in our society, that is our present educational system," by doing a better job of teaching students to read and appreciate reading.

Blouke planned "to eliminate Progressive Education and to provide a much broader and more academically oriented education for each child." But the struggle that actually took place over the next three decades proved different. On one side, Blouke's own textbooks developed in less easily categorized ways than anyone – himself included – might have predicted in 1962. Neither spontaneous exploration nor rote drills could achieve his goals for students. On the other side, the education culture had developed its own institutional inertia, in which catch-phrases from either side might be used to justify practices which had become self-perpetuating.

Educational historian Larry Cuban offers a useful metaphor in his book *How Teachers Taught: Constancy and Change in American Classrooms 1880–1990,* though he employs it a bit differently. "Hurricane winds sweep across the sea, tossing up 20-foot waves; a fathom below the surface turbulent waters swirl, while on an ocean floor there is unruffled calm." A new idea in education may bring forth a storm. "Professional journals, for example, echo arguments for and against a new theory. Letters to editors and sharp rebuttals add to the flurry. Books are written and reputations are made. Conferences host both skeptics and promoters. Professors of education teach the new wisdom to their students. Some school boards adopt policies and start an occasional program consistent with the novel concept." But down on the ocean floor, silence reigns. "Most publishers continue producing texts barely touched by the new theory and most teachers use methods unmarked by either controversy or slogans."

Thus educational routines long outlive any justification they may once have had. As Open Court education director Carl Bereiter wrote in the mid-1980s, grammar drill (for instance) "has no significant advocates" among researchers of any persuasion. "It is simply an institutionalized practice that survives for a variety of reasons that have nothing to do with instructional theory." It will take more than a surface storm to rearrange the ocean floor. Reformers have to work down at that level.

"Our programs were inspired by the same idealism as the government-sponsored curriculum projects of the 60s," Blouke reflected a quarter-century later. "Unlike those projects, our programs have grown and prospered and made a real difference in the classroom. That is because we took teachers' needs into account, and field tested the programs carefully before publishing them." Open Court was never prosperous; it often perceived teachers' needs differently from the way teachers did; and it didn't always field test as much as it claimed. But even with these qualifications, it did bring radical ideas into many thousands of classrooms. Many children, especially in disadvantaged neighborhoods of large cities, learned to read, who probably would not have without Open Court. Many thousands of teachers found they could accomplish things they never thought possible with such children. By showing that they *were* possible, the company contributed to the gradual rise in expectations of the schools. These are arguably deeper and more lasting educational changes than anything CBE or similar groups could have accomplished by staying on the surface trying to blow up a bigger hurricane.

3. Ahead of its time: the beginnings of Open Court reading (1962–1967)

"Teachers have given far too many fill-the-blanks lessons, yes and no tests, and multiple-choice quizzes. . . . thousands of dollars are being spent for seat work which is useless and even detrimental. It is appalling that workbooks have become blanket assignments to keep the children busy! . . . The child's work must take the place of the workbook, furnishing the material for which he actually has a need."
– Nellie Thomas, *"Let the Children Do the Work: English Handbook for Teachers,"* 1962

PHONICS FOR LITERATURE

CRITIQUE IS EASY, construction hard. Bestor, Flesch, and Trace inspired Blouke with their attacks on the American curriculum of the 1950s. But they didn't tell him how to improve on it. Nor did existing alternatives offer a useful model. *Rodnaya Rech* was too foreign; the McGuffey Readers, in Blouke's eyes, were "dripping with morality" and lacking in modern science.

The Open Court reading program was therefore constructed piecemeal, from an unlikely mix of ingredients, by an incongruous and occasionally incompatible half-dozen helpers: three very different teachers, a college English professor, a German émigré, and a researcher working for a fringe phonics group. Blouke's relentless networking brought them together. Without benefit of the federal funds then being dispensed to university-based curriculum reformers, his engineering cast of mind turned their disparate efforts into a coherent product. "He would read two stories," his wife recalls of a later joint effort, "and say, 'These should be working together.'"

The first step from critique to construction was short. Blouke

27

called up Arther Trace and asked him to help develop the kind of textbooks he had called for in *What Ivan Knows that Johnny Doesn't*. Trace said he couldn't spare the time. Later, when Blouke called back wondering whom he should ask instead, Trace agreed to help find or write high-quality stories for a series of elementary readers. The two quickly agreed that only a small publisher could be expected to bring about the needed changes.

Of course, good stories would have little value if the kids couldn't read them. To bring students in touch with the best of Western and world cultures, Open Court had to teach reading quickly and efficiently, without the stultifying vocabulary restrictions look-say methods required. That meant phonics. Blouke adopted it for pragmatic reasons, not ideology. "As an engineer I wanted to include what worked." He would have employed any beginning-reading method that could lead students promptly to literature.

Even in 1962, with the look-say method at the height of educational fashion, a few phonics-based approaches to reading were available. The most popular was published by the Economy Company, with which Blouke was familiar because a version of it had shared the spotlight with Dick and Jane in André's first-grade classroom. Family friend Priscilla McQueen, who had worked with Mildred McGinnis teaching aphasic children, pointed out its flaw. "It had 110–120 different 'keys,'" recalls Blouke, "which are abstract rules that don't work, especially for vowels."

Instead, he and McQueen worked together to develop a phonics sequence for beginners using two techniques. Noah Webster's diacritical marks established the one-to-one sound-to-symbol correspondence lacking in normal written English, and had some similarity to the International Teaching Alphabet (ITA), which Blouke had once investigated. Mildred McGinnis's Association Method bypassed rules by associating each sound with a picture of an action creating it. This was a key point, one rarely grasped by anti-phonics authors, who assume that any phonics program must involve rules. Since McGinnis's own book, *Aphasic Children*, had not yet been published, McQueen's experience of working under her was crucial. (Larry Cuban writes in *How*

Teachers Taught that educators often blunt fundamental reforms by encapsulating them in ancillary programs for special populations, away from the mainstream classrooms. In the case of Open Court, ideas flowed the opposite way, from the margins toward the center.)

Blouke and McQueen worked to meld these sources into a primer and teacher's guide that could be used in the classroom. To establish the key association between sounds and print, they created 43 wall sound cards (later renamed sound-spelling cards). Each displayed the common spelling(s) of a sound along with a picture of some activity *producing* the sound. Thus the sound "b" was represented by a bass drum (rather than a ball) and the unvoiced "s" by a hissing teakettle (rather than a swing). Each day the teacher was to introduce one sound and its common spellings.

"Rather than learn abstract phonetic rules, . . . this method emphasizes learning-by-doing," Blouke wrote in the foreword to *Reading Is Fun,* the first Open Court reader, published in 1963. "The children hear the sound, they see or read the sound, they say the sound aloud, and they write the sound." The company called this a "multi-modal approach." Decades later, we can see that Open Court was accommodating the practical teacher's insight that different children learn in different ways – but without losing sight of the fact that there are some things they all need to learn.

Open Court was also ahead of its time in embracing another of McGinnis's recommendations: don't group students by ability. "It is better to teach the entire class together so that each child may profit by observing the others," she wrote in *Aphasic Children.* Classmates making individual sounds and blending them together in unison became one hallmark of a well-run Open Court first grade. Work in the whole-class setting helped slower students keep up, and spared them the social stigma of being assigned to low-ability "loser" reading groups.

Whole-class work in Open Court did not hide individuals in a regimented mass. Blouke was determined "to build feedback into every activity so that students can correct themselves and teachers know where the students are." The 1965 teacher's guide described the response-card game, in which each child has a set of cards, one for each sound learned. When the teacher asked to see a particular sound, each child was to hold up the appropriate card – enabling the teacher to see at a glance how well the lessons had been learned.

These instant feedback mechanisms worked well and were also ahead of their time. In the early 1980s, when everyone was asking about computerized instruction, the company was able to give a pat answer: "What do computers do that the pre-electronic classroom didn't do? They are interactive, they give instantaneous feedback. Open Court's entire pedagogy has been based on a system of instantaneous feedback (evident in the games, the response devices, the composition cycle, and other areas) for 20 years." (This answer, which seems so cogent now, satisfied no one at the time. Says André Carus, "They wanted worksheets on a computer screen," not a new pedagogy.)

Despite its ultimate goal, Open Court's text for the first semester of first grade, *We Can Read*, did not contain great literature. The reading matter had to be tailored to give students practice in associating particular sounds with particular print characters. Thus Lesson 10-D focused single-mindedly on "p," long "i," and long "e" – "I see a pipe. See Pete eat pie" – sounds already introduced, so that students could decode them. Toward the end of the primer, when the students had mastered enough sounds, they read "Peter Piper Picked a Peck of Pickled Peppers" (Lesson 42-D) and "Little Miss Muffet" (Lesson 51-C-4).

This feature of Open Court and other phonics-based readers has its analogue in reading textbooks based on the whole-word approach. They famously use near-nonsense repetition ("See! See Spot run! Run, run, run! See Spot jump! Jump, jump, jump! See Spot run and jump!") so that students can memorize what entire words look like, and guess at others from pictures or context. Both phonics and look-say approaches require some artificial practice of a technique, and to that extent neither one can be faulted for presenting odd or boring text at the beginning rather than good literature. The difference lies in the value of the technique being practiced. Open Court students were able to move beyond phonics practice after only a few months, because they had learned the code and could figure out unfamiliar words on their own.

Where could Blouke try out the new beginning reader? He had few contacts in the schools and his approach was not calculated to develop many. "As soon as I mentioned Flesch, they'd get all red in the face." He finally appealed to George Lorentz, André's camp counselor in Wisconsin, who was also principal of McKinley School in Harvey, a suburb south of Chicago. Lorentz was not a convert, but he was willing to help. He introduced Blouke to an open-minded teacher, and for about three months in the fall of 1962, McQueen Integrated Phonics was taught in Mrs. Norris's first grade there. Both Blouke and McQueen visited her classroom, and revised their work repeatedly as the year went on.

Exposure to classroom reality strengthened Blouke's confidence. "I am fully convinced that this is by far the best learning-to-read method there is," he wrote to Richard Dennis, president of the Great Books Foundation, in April 1963. "We have done our best to make it idiot-proof, so that the teachers, or even interested parents, can teach six-year-olds to read very quickly and with confidence. The selections Dr. Trace has made should then prepare the students for great reading fluency by the end of third grade."

READINGS "WHICH GOOD TASTE AND TRADITION HAVE CHOSEN TO PRESERVE"

Basic phonics had to be brief, because for Blouke it was only the means to an end. He wanted the mechanics of reading taught quickly and thoroughly so that students could move on to more valuable texts. In the earliest years of school, Blouke wanted students to become acquainted with "the literature of their appropriate age level which good taste and tradition have chosen to preserve. . . . A special effort has been made to exclude from these readers any selections which are inane, trivial, dull, or otherwise unrewarding."

Thus Open Court anticipated the vogue for genuine literature that "whole language" teachers espoused decades later. Acceptable selections proved hard to find, however, with quality nonfiction especially scarce. Trace found some and wrote some, but as they moved beyond first grade Blouke came to feel he needed a greater variety of selections. Finally he appealed for help to his wife Marianne – already fully occupied with three children under the age of ten – "and discovered what a wonderful editor I had married!"

Marianne was well qualified in that she had studied literature in college and read a great deal herself as a child, and again to her children. "The true classics of children's literature have as much to offer to adults as to children and are read with equal enthusiasm by both," she told a company workshop in 1966. "If a parent becomes bored with reading a book out loud to his child, there must be something wrong with the book."

She was not so well qualified in that most of the stories she was familiar with were German, she had never learned to type, and neither she nor Blouke had been trained in writing or editing. They compensated with passion and determination. They brainstormed together, edited each other, and tried the results out on their own children. One day in 1966 a company salesman called about the almost-finished fourth-grade reader: "Marianne, I have to have a name for the book right away! We have an order for them from Rockford, and the book just has to have a name for the order blank!" She and Blouke spent the evening filling sheet after sheet with possible names before they found their title phrase "what joy awaits you" in Wordsworth's "To a Butterfly."

Back in the 1950s, when Blouke had been absorbed in inventing more efficient ways to make potassium permanganate, he couldn't bring work home with him. Now that Marianne was involved, the textbooks became part of their partnership. "We more or less identified with the Open Court Program as if it were our own 4th, 5th, 6th, 7th, 8th, 9th, 10th, 11th and 12th child." Soon there was no surface in the house to eat on. Papers blanketed the kitchen table, the dining-room table, the coffee table, the kitchen counters, and every other flat surface. The rest of the family's life had to fit into the leftover space.

Their motivation was moral as well as intellectual. Throughout the company's existence Blouke monitored selections with character-building in mind. In 1986 he insisted on using the original version of the "Three Little Pigs," in which the first two young pigs are eaten by the wolf. "The whole story loses its main point if there are no serious consequences for the first two pigs' laziness and neglect of duty," he advised a subordinate. "You may think I am crazy, but I still remember rather vividly when I heard this story at four or five. . . . I am certain that we will lose some customers because they don't like the so-called violence. . . . But I also feel that we will probably win an equal number of customers for not pandering to the very dangerous attitude that is gnawing at our society, that there are no consequences for laziness, irresponsibility, and 'doing your own thing.'"

END RUN

Students using the 1963 *Reading Is Fun* (typically in the second semester of first grade) read Aesop's fables ("The Fox and the Grapes," "The Hare and the Tortoise," "The Boy Who Cried Wolf"); Mother Goose rhymes; folk tales ("The Little Red Hen," "The Gingerbread Boy," "The Three Billy Goats Gruff," "The Three Bears"); and poems by Vachel Lindsay, Robert Louis Stevenson, and Christina Rosetti. At least half of the fifty-six selections can be easily identified as classics. By comparison, Scott, Foresman's best-selling 1952 reader for the first semester of second grade contained just seven folk tales out of its 48 selections, and these had to be watered down because of the books' extremely restricted vocabulary.

That spring Blouke used the media to continue his end run around the education establishment. He mailed a preliminary brochure and copies of the new readers to several dozen newspaper contacts who had reviewed *What Ivan Knows that Johnny Doesn't*. Four of the recipients reviewed the new series favorably. "Dick and Jane are bores . . . . [and] moral neuters," wrote syndicated columnist John Chamberlain in the September 10, 1963, *New York Journal-American*. It was too late to go back to McGuffey, Chamberlain continued, but "there are good modern readers being published, such as the series now being put out by the Open Court Publishing Company of LaSalle, Ill."

In the fall of 1963, eight schools, scattered from Spokane to Boston, tried it out. Experience in these classrooms confirmed the value of the wall sound cards. It also showed that the essential step of blending individual sounds together into words was harder than expected. Teachers had to practice blending with students systematically, daily, and in unison. According to Blouke, "One third can do it instantly. For another third it takes a while. And the last third takes three months. The unison carries them along without embarrassment. I visited eight classrooms in 1963, and the teachers said everyone had learned it by January. No kids were left behind."

The 1963 trials also showed that Open Court could be effective with disadvantaged children, further expanding Blouke's vision for the program: "If underprivileged children can be taught to read well and with enthusiasm and to write independently in the first grade, one of the main educational problems in the ghettos of America can be eliminated." By September 1964, an expanded "Open Court Multi-Sensory Reading and Composition" program was in 323 schools.

ADDING WORKSHOP

"Never in all my years of teaching first grade (28 classes of first graders) have I experienced the joy of seeing *all* my pupils read," said Sister Annunciata, also known as Sister Lucille Bernier, of the Holy Family School in Orange, California, after teaching one of the 1963 classrooms. She spread the word in southern California, working as a part-time consultant for the company, and she proposed an addition to the program that Blouke welcomed.

Bernier's "workshop" drew on her Montessori background. This part of the Open Court classroom day was intended as a counterpoint to whole-class work – "a time of independent, self-chosen reading activities." Students were to work independently or in small groups, using materials that "lend themselves to activities which children can carry on alone with success more often than with failure and mistakes – activities with a built-in control of error." These were said to include dictionaries, reference books, vocabulary cards, reading matter for "enrichment," self-correcting worksheets, flash cards, and puzzles. By 1972, Open Court's workshop kit had grown to include anagrams, movable alphabets, tracing paper, alphabet paper, word-matching games, and phonograph records.

"After planning the environment for creative individual Language Arts activities, the teacher must have the courage to step aside long enough to observe what her children can do," Bernier wrote in a 1970 teacher's guide. Workshop can be seen as a variant of the progressive idea that the classroom is a society in miniature where students learn to be self-directed, responsible, and cooperative.

Open Court workshop periods were also supposed to give the teacher time to provide extra help to students who needed it, without confining them to a fixed group of "slow learners." Flexible grouping, not tracking, was key. The remaining students could work independently or in groups with materials at their own levels. Workshop also aided in the education of boys, a concern prominent in the 1960s that has grown less fashionable since. As Sister Lucille told the *Los Angeles Times* in a July 1968 interview, "Boys don't like to come to school for school is a place where they have to sit. But they like it when [using Open Court] they are able to choose their materials freely, work independently and be able to read so soon."

Workshop was the least traditional element of Open Court, and it proved to be among the hardest to explain to classroom teachers. They often ignored it or treated it as a time to hand out pages of busy work. In 1984, when Marsha Roit visited Open Court classrooms in West Virginia, she saw "little evidence of its use as a procedure to develop independence or to reinforce skills. In many cases, workshop was nothing more than 10 minutes spent on games that required little thought. Seldom was there any small group work by the teacher."

Open Court's persistent inability to get teachers to incorporate Workshop into their routines was especially unfortunate. Without it, whole-class instruction could not work as efficiently.

When Steven Stahl of the University of Illinois evaluated the Open Court program and observed classes in 1990, Workshop remained hard to grasp. "It is only after talking with a number of Open Court personnel that I have an idea of what is to be done in workshop. None of the teachers in McCosh had a clue. . . . None of the teachers I saw used it, at all. Instead, they kept the whole class at the lowest common level."

This experience is also a clue that Open Court's fight was against the inertia of the education culture, not against "progressivism" as Blouke at first thought. If progressive ideology had really dominated school life, Workshop would have been recognized and welcomed, not ignored.

ADDING WRITING

"Workbooks have become one of the greatest drawbacks to a successful English program," wrote Nellie Thomas of Rockford, Illinois, in a 1962 guide for English teachers. "*The child's work*" – that is, writing – "must take the place of the workbook, furnishing the material for which he actually has a need." Having seen Romalda Spalding's *The Writing Road to Reading*, Blouke was prepared for the idea that writing should be part of the curriculum from the beginning. A 1963 newspaper article alerted him and Marianne to Thomas, who was then supervisor of composition and reading in the Lincoln Park school district outside Rockford, Illinois. Within months she was adapting for Open Court her "praise and pressure" system of teaching writing, including student proofreading – hence her slogan, "let the children do the work."

Thomas's own teaching style was unabashedly emotional and personal and focused on children's interests, but she distanced herself from progressive education as she had seen it practiced. "Unless a classroom becomes a workshop of relaxed, stabilized, and quiet children," she wrote, "there will not be learning. A relaxed classroom must not be confused with a disorderly and undisciplined one! . . . misinterpretations of the basic philosophy of progressive education led to a cult of pseudo-progressives who embraced the theory that teachers destroyed the interest of children with formal discipline." In the classroom, Thomas combined concern with children's emotional lives with a demand for real work, as in her proposal for motivating student compositions:

"A teacher must dare to be different! She must pull away from monotonous repetition of, 'Today we are going to write a story.' Most children view that announcement with exactly what it deserves, and there are few teachers who are not aware of what the reactions are.

"Emotion is the key which unlocks the minds of so many boys and girls, and helps to release the potential ability lying dormant, and too often wasted. . . . It is only when a teacher is able to share her own experiences and emotions with her class, that she will be able to guide those children into sharing their emotions with her. And when they do, they will lose the inhibitions which have stifled the expression of any inner thought.

"When the teacher chooses a title for a written paragraph without considering the child's interests, she can expect complete disinterest in return. But if she is able to share honestly and sincerely her own feelings with him, the child will in return feel free to share his feelings honestly and sincerely with her. And when he is free to do this, he has a purpose for writing!

"Picture this. A teacher enters the room after her class has assembled. As usual, she stands quietly before her class, her hands behind her back. Unexpectedly and without introduction or explanation, she tells her students of some fearful experience which she has had. The subject of *Fear* is an abstract but a common human emotion and will catch the interest of most children.

"The abruptness and sincerity with which the teacher speaks creates the impact necessary to shock the student out of his mental apathy.

"He is oblivious to the fact that this is a classroom, and he forgets that the speaker is a teacher, and he is a student. It is merely the sharing of an experience with another person."

Open Court also took up Thomas's process of isolating specific sentences for whole-class revision, which became known as "sentence lifting." As some of the company's later promotional materials boasted, "The self-correcting technique teaches students to accept the responsibility for their own learning" – the seedling of Open Court's later interest in encouraging higher-order independent thinking.

Thomas had students post their improved work on the wall next to earlier efforts. "This continuous posting of improved papers is the great motivation which keeps the child always reaching up toward better work," she wrote. "All improvement must come willingly from the child; it must not be forced through the constant reminder of the teacher!" This was consonant with Blouke's long-standing insistence on positive rewards.

"It was very unconventional to allow mistakes in a program," Blouke recalls, "but it worked. Kids don't become sensitive to proofreading unless they have to deal with errors." Once again, Open Court anticipated the good aspects of a later fashion – invented spelling – without the excess that would allow it to continue indefinitely. Instead Thomas offered a strategy by which students could learn to correct and revise their own work.

Actually, it was unconventional to have real writing in the program at all. In 1964 the executive secretary of the National Council of Teachers of English called writing "the disgrace of American education"; and in 1985 little had changed in mainstream classrooms. "Children spend very little time in writing activities" in typical first-, third-, and fifth-grade classrooms, observed Connie Bridge and Elfrieda Hiebert in the *Elementary School Journal*. And even most of that time was not spent in writing, but in "transcription activities that involve verbatim copying of other writers' texts. Students seldom compose discourse-level texts, and they rarely write for a real audience. Language arts textbooks do not suggest and teachers rarely use prewriting activities to stimulate children's thinking prior to writing. Teachers neglect opportunities to relate writing to ongoing activities in the classroom." Open Court remained ahead of its time for a long time.

Blouke credits Nellie Thomas with converting Open Court from a phonics-plus-literature program to "a complete integrated language arts program – broader than any other." But his own contribution was equally indispensable if less visible – namely, realizing that writing belonged there from the very beginning.

"The first writing I ever did was in seventh grade," he recalls. "It was painful. But when we started it in first grade, students took to it like a duck to water."

RESEARCH?

One source Blouke drew on sparingly as the program developed was educational research. Most such research was of course conducted by people who would have been biased against Open Court's goals and methods alike. Furthermore, the Council for Basic Education took a dim view of educational research, on the grounds that "Education is not yet a science and the good teacher remains an artist dependent on insight and common sense." (In this view CBE followed turn-of-the-century academics like Harvard President Charles W. Eliot, who according to Ellen Condliffe Lagemann "prized good teaching, but were not at all sanguine that education could benefit from systematic investigation.")

There is a germ of truth in this sentiment. Even good research does not specify how to implement favored procedures. It's one thing to know, for instance, that direct instruction works best; it's quite another to know exactly when to teach and what to say. As André Carus pointed out in 1984, "It is impossible to 'base' an entire program on research. Research results are fragmentary and limited; a curriculum, by definition, is comprehensive. It is the job of the Open Court curriculum author to create a program that makes the content we want to teach as interesting as possible. In steering this course, research results are like slalom gates; they are constraints on the task, not its ultimate purpose." Science sets boundaries, but curriculum-making remains an art and a craft.

In any case, in the early 1960s Blouke would have had trouble finding any slalom gates at all. What passed as educational research in those days was an intellectual wasteland. There were few controlled empirical studies of the kind normally associated with the word "research"; where they existed he was happy to take advantage of them. Louise Gurren and Ann Hughes published what may have been the first careful review and meta-analysis of twenty-two studies of phonics in the April 1965 issue of the *Journal of Educational Research.* This journal claimed to be "dedicated to the scientific study of education," but of the remaining eight articles in that issue, only one rose above the level of simple description. In March 1966, when Hughes and others published results of Open Court's Hegeler Project in *Instructor,* that magazine (more likely to be read by classroom teachers) also published a special supplement supposedly presenting results of research in language arts. Only two of the ten articles in the supplement even attempted to match and compare control and experimental groups, and they did so very imprecisely. Open Court's research – printed elsewhere in the magazine and not included in that supplement – stood out as far more rigorous than the norm.

Hughes then worked for the Reading Reform Foundation, which was less fanatically pro-phonics then than it later became. She was herself impressed by the Hegeler Project results (see next chapter). When Blouke and McQueen fell out in 1965, Hughes agreed to rewrite the first-grade program in a matter of months. Her version blended Montessori, Bernier, Thomas, and McGinnis, and remained the framework for Open Court reading and writing until the 1990s.

DIRECT TEACHING AND DISCOVERY LEARNING

Open Court grew out of the reaction against progressive education, but it did not in fact seek to replace the current educational fashion with traditional orthodoxy. Even at this early date, the company's curriculum had moved beyond the rhetoric of Flesch and Trace and the Council for Basic Education. By appealing to different learning styles, by not grouping students according to ability, by providing good literature, by encouraging writing and proofreading, by fostering self-directed learning in writing and in workshop, the company in the mid-1960s had more in common with good educational practice of the 1990s and beyond than it did with the McGuffey Readers. Within its core principles, it reflected Blouke's willingness to use whatever worked.

Ann Hughes exemplified this practical approach. In a 1966 in-service program, she carefully distinguished the stages of teaching first-graders a new sound. The teacher, she explained, "has the children listen to the new sound, say it, see how it is spelled, and write it. Then she gives them the chance to use this new piece of knowledge in discovering words for themselves. Notice that she used direct teaching for teaching the sound itself," and then reinforced it by having children engage in other activities. "After this initial direct teaching, the approach becomes a discovery one as the children use the new sound to figure out new words" – words new to their reading vocabulary, but already familiar in spoken form.

All this was in contrast to mainstream publishers' phonics programs where students are expected to learn basic sound-spelling correspondences by "discovery learning" (or induction) from seeing a large number of them. Blouke had created a system in which both stereotypically traditionalist and progressive methods worked in tandem for the children.

This quality of the Open Court program was a substantive strength and a marketing weakness. It required teachers to be conversant with a variety of methods. And the program worked best when used *as a system* (thus the common omission of Workshop dragged down the level of whole-class instruction). Teachers accustomed to trying a little of this and a little of that were likely to be put off by an approach that did not lend itself to tinkering.

"I feel this program must be handled by a firm teacher to obtain good results," one teacher wrote in response to a 1968 questionnaire. "It is not a program that can be taught one day & forgotten the next." Similarly, Ervin Nephew of Cypress, California, told Blouke, "We're having to re-educate teachers [to] a different way of thinking. . . . The teachers we have the most problem with are the teachers who think they know the most about reading and have had the most experience." Blouke succeeded in much, but he did not create a program that anyone could teach right from the book. Without intensive training followed by constant vigilance and supervision, it was susceptible to misuse and abandonment.

REVOLUTION FROM BELOW

As the program grew, so did Blouke's enthusiasm. He came to

believe that improvement in the beginning years of school would force upgrading throughout. "Our objective," he wrote in the late 1960s, "is to develop a textbook program which, given reasonably competent teachers, will enable students to receive a broad liberal arts education, similar to a German Gymnasium or French Lycée, by the time of graduation from high school." Since "second-graders using the new program should read at about the fourth-grade level, . . . this would indeed open up all kinds of possibilities for upgrading instruction for *all* of the other subjects." He had the same ambition in mathematics: "We intend to gain two years by the end of sixth grade primarily by making the program more interesting for teachers and students and by involving each child more actively." Students who had been through such a program would want better than they were getting in subsequent grades. As they grew, they would destroy the empire of the educators from below.

But what of those administrators who would not countenance even a toothless citizens' committee? They would hardly welcome an engineer intent on revamping their entire curriculum without benefit of credentials. Blouke hoped to render them irrelevant. Open Court would simply "by-pass those committed to look-say and Dick and Jane, and to those young educators who are open-minded we could point to success in the classroom, eliminating the need for useless argument."

This did happen sometimes. In Richmond, Virginia, in 1966–67, one first-grade teacher couldn't buy Open Court books because the state had not adopted the program and therefore would not pay for them. She "wanted so badly to use 1:1 with her first graders that she taught the entire course from the board," Ann Hughes reported. "I said, 'Didn't the children mind not having books?' Mrs. Hill smiled and said, 'They didn't know there *were* books.'"

Throughout its history Open Court rarely drew a tepid response, and for every story like this there were others of disdain and inertia. About the same time as the Richmond teacher was doing it all herself, company consultant Leila Mustachi was observing a Washington, D.C., teacher who "still has children who do not know the alphabet but her workshop kit was UNOPENED. AAAAARGHHH. She kills time by giving the *slow* children colouring & busy-work and the few times she has the extra-prac. session it is listening to the best ones read! The ones who need it never get it." A Brooklyn teacher told Mustachi that her second-graders could not read, only memorize. "I went to the board and put the words 'crime,' 'Greece' and several others on it – ones that they had not read in their books and the children sounded them out perfectly. 'Can you say the children memorized these?' I asked her. She conceded that they couldn't have but refuses to admit that they could learn."

Even as Blouke put together the first Open Court program, Richard Hofstadter was writing what could have been a direct and prophetic warning: "Professional education is still largely staffed, at the administrative levels and in its centers of training, by people who are far from enthusiastic about the new demand for academic excellence. American education is in a position somewhat like that of a new political regime which must depend for the execution of its mandates upon a civil service honeycombed with determined opponents." Blouke's position was even more precarious than that. He was trying to sell academically excellent textbooks to functionaries in that civil service.

Mere success in the classroom, it soon appeared, would not win Open Court enough support to transform the dominant culture of education. Open Court's classroom success would either be ignored or discounted, forcing Blouke and his followers into decades of struggle. Rather than eliminate "the need for useless argument," as he had hoped, success would provide occasion for even more.

4. Selling reform with guarantees (1966–1973)

"Before I started representing publishers, I used to represent distributors of bulldozers, cranes, hand shovels – [selling] all kinds of construction equipment. I called on bricklayers and guys who were building interstate highways. Sometimes I'd be standing in two inches of mud, sometimes in two inches of carpet. A guy would want a crane that was able to lift X amount of weight in X amount of radius. He'd say, 'Tell us how your equipment meets those challenges.' I have yet to have public school people ask me that kind of question." – Whyte Ellington, June 19, 2000

BRIDGING THE GAP

AT THE BEGINNING of 1967, Open Court was running six-figure annual deficits and threatening to consume the assets of its sponsor, the Hegeler Foundation. So the foundation sold Open Court to Carus Chemical in return for chemical company shares. The tax savings from the transfer financed the textbook company's start. Now a private enterprise in structure as well as in spirit, Open Court would have to respond to the educational market in order to survive long enough to reform it.

It started fast. Open Court's nationwide sales doubled from $600,000 in 1967 to $1.25 million in 1969, and kept growing at about 25 percent a year in the early 1970s, when the company claimed 10 percent of all first-grade classrooms. In September 1966, the company had eighteen "demonstration centers" where curious teachers could come and see the program in action. Four years later it had 119, in thirty-five states. Its product line burgeoned from a first-grade phonics primer into a full-scale program that combined reading, spelling, writing, and literature for kindergarten through sixth grade; a remedial reading program; and nascent math, science, and music programs.

This growth did not come easily. First responses from potential customers were often uncomprehending. In the spring of 1965 Open Court exhibited its wares, as did other textbook vendors, at a major gathering of reading teachers, the annual meeting of the International Reading Association (IRA). The IRA was the product of a 1956 merger between the International Council for the Improvement of Reading Instruction and the National Association for Remedial Teaching. Its first president had been William S. Gray, author of Scott, Foresman's Dick and Jane reading series. The IRA remained as it had begun – an influential voice of orthodoxy in elementary reading instruction. The nature of that orthodoxy in the spring of 1965 can be gauged from the response Blouke and Marianne got.

"Teachers would come by and ask, 'What is this?'" recalls Marianne. "'A literature program for fourth-graders,' I would say. *'Literature?'* They were scared. They thought literature was only for adults. Stories were for kids.

"We talked nonstop for three days. He talked about phonics and I talked about literature. We both lost our voices."

School-board member and former teacher Susan MacBride faced a similar challenge when she volunteered to bring Open Court's message to the Maine and New Hampshire teachers' conventions in October 1966. She attracted attention by displaying stories written by Open Court first graders. But when she asked teachers to sign up for more information, many declined. "A few said they might lose their jobs, or be laughed at by their superiors or that they felt it was fruitless, so ingrained was Scott, Foresman, etc." Worse than fear of retribution was simple disbelief that students could do the work Open Court demanded. "Every single person who saw our materials said they were too advanced for their respective grade level at present."

Throughout its existence, most teachers did see Open Court's program as being impossibly difficult. They could not take seriously the idea that first-graders, let alone inner-city first graders, could read fables from Aesop or poems by Robert Louis Stevenson. But they did.

"I don't think you could find more amazing results anywhere in the country," Open Court consultant and former teacher Leila Mustachi reported after visiting Washington School in New Brunswick, New Jersey, in the spring of 1968 – "and this is a deprived area, heterogeneous [first-grade] class! They have finished 'Reading is Fun.' 10 out of the 27 in the class are reading the 3rd grade Ginn [another publisher's] reader. The others, except for 2 or 3 retarded pupils, are reading the 2nd grade Ginn reader (2:2). They are writing compositions, consuming library books, reading newspapers – in short, knocking everyone cold. Mrs. Sander says that she feels she wasted her previous 5 years in the classroom."

How to reach those who couldn't or wouldn't visit these classrooms? A ringing call for liberal-arts education comparable to a German *Gymnasium* would not sell most American educators. Blouke and Marianne had to translate their high-minded goal into slogans – "all your students can read," or Nellie Thomas's "let the children do the work" – and then find out which ones would resonate within the education culture they sought to transform.

Blouke pursued strategies that came naturally to him – systematically comparing Open Court results with those of other programs, and offering to guarantee those results in various ways. He also continued to seek out new helpers, making forays into every imaginable geographic and ideological quarter of the country. At various times over the years, he corresponded with, or was in pursuit of, Phyllis Schlafly, Mel and Norma Gabler, Marva Collins, Jesse Jackson, and Nixon Administration staffers.. Nor did he take fright easily when help came from unexpected quarters, as described in the following two chapters. Of the company's early consultants, the most effective proved to be a North Dakotan who coupled an emotional, almost revivalistic, appeal with intensive teacher training. Later, when Blouke picked an advisory board composed largely of prestigious educational traditionalists, the most influential in the long run proved to be the youngest and least conservative.

These recruitments and experiments changed and deepened the Open Court idea, just as the contributions of Nellie Thomas and Sister Annunciata had. It remained Blouke's idea, but he had to let it grow beyond what he could have made it on his own.

SELLING WITH DATA

Blouke's own idea of a conversion experience was a new set of data. As an engineer, he knew the value of controlled experiments. He wanted to compare two groups of students who would be as similar as possible – in IQ, socio-economic background, proportion of boys and girls, teacher training and experience. One group would use Open Court, the other not. For this task, he was able to recruit Ann Hughes to work with a few professionals on what became known as the "Hegeler Project."

The Hegeler Project was ahead of its time both in its careful design and in its focus on children attending schools in "disadvantaged" areas. "Most publishers and most researchers shy away from experiments involving children of low IQ because it is pleasanter to present high scores," Hughes wrote in November 1964, "and the easiest way to get high scores is to start with children of higher IQ. Yet it is the disadvantaged children who need the most help and provide the severest test of any materials. Naturally, they should be compared with control children of similar IQ. Comparisons of this sort are not only fair, they are long overdue."

In its first year, the project tested the achievement of 704 first graders using Open Court. Their results were compared with those of 717 children of similar IQs in the same nine school systems who were using Scott, Foresman, and similar look-say textbooks. Ann Hughes and Nellie Thomas summarized the results in the March 1966 issue of *Instructor* magazine under the title "Beginning Reading for Disadvantaged Children." The Open Court students performed better across the board. They were able to read at levels achieved only by non-Open-Court pupils with IQs 20 points higher. (Results were statistically significant, with only a 1 percent likelihood of their being due to chance.) Non-readers made up 18 percent of the control children but only 6 percent of the Open Court children.

As we have seen in chapter 3, the Hegeler Project's methods compared favorably with those of contemporary educational studies. But skeptics could always discount it as a self-interested company sales aid, and for both financial and logistical reasons it was not continued for several years as originally planned. Thus it measured only the company's introductory phonics program, not its later-grade offerings. In later years the company tried to develop more data, but never matched this first effort, as Blouke acknowledged in 1983. "Although our *Headway* and *Real Math* programs produce the best results in terms of standardized tests, we do not have high quality research studies to document this."

Extra data might not have made much difference, though. Far more prestigious studies made little impression on the education culture.

In 1967, Harvard professor Jeanne Chall published *Reading: The Great Debate,* in which she systematically reviewed more than 200 studies of beginning reading. Blouke called it "probably the most important book on reading instruction that has ever been published" and claimed that it made phonics "respectable." Open Court workshops drew more people after the book appeared. But since Chall's findings did not conform to IRA orthodoxy or conventional classroom practice, her book won little respect among professional educators – a fate worth examining in detail since Open Court faced the same kind of opposition. (Blouke recalls that Chall paid a personal price as well; she told him that she lost half of her friends when the book came out.)

The methods used in the studies Chall had to work with left much to be desired. Most authors "did not indicate how the experimental and control groups were selected, how much time was allotted to various aspects of reading, how the teachers were selected, whether the quality of the teaching was comparable in both groups, or even whether teachers followed the methods under study. Even more important, most studies did not specify clearly what a 'method' involved, but instead merely assigned labels (e.g., 'phonics'), expecting the reader to understand what was meant." Worse, many researchers drew conclusions that seemed to go counter to their own findings, forcing Chall to analyze their studies more carefully than they themselves had.

Chall was nevertheless able to bring together three heretofore separate strands of research bearing on early reading: controlled experimental studies in laboratory or classroom, classroom correlational studies, and clinical studies of reading failure. Together, they led her to endorse the intensive early teaching of phonics, a technique central to Open Court's program. (The company itself had asked to be omitted from the book for two reasons. Blouke was in the midst of changing from the McQueen to the Hughes primer and did not want the McQueen edition mentioned; and company scuttlebutt erroneously had it that Chall's book was not going to be sympathetic.)

The existing research, Chall wrote, tended to confirm that "the first step in learning to read in one's native language is essentially learning a printed code for the speech we possess. It does not support the prevailing view that sees the beginning reader as a miniature adult who should, from the start, engage in mature reading." Indeed, teaching based on that view might well produce more serious failures than emphasizing the code. Most congenial to Blouke's ears, "There is some experimental evidence that children of below-average and average intelligence and children of lower socioeconomic background do better with an early code emphasis."

Chall debunked some of Flesch's extreme claims for phonics. "The experimental research provides no evidence that either a code or a meaning emphasis fosters greater love of reading or is more interesting to children." If Dick and Jane were bores, it was only to the parents.

Professional educators responded less judiciously to *Reading: The Great Debate.* Writing in the *Reading Teacher,* Ruth Strang of the University of Arizona, coauthor of *The Improvement of Reading,* first criticized Chall for a "destructively critical attitude" in treating the matter as a debate – and then proceeded to debate her. "To begin with the synthetic or code-emphasis method," Strang wrote, "may 1) decrease the child's initial curiosity about printed words as he encounters and uses them, 2) deprive him of the experience of discovering sound-symbol relationships in words for himself [, and] 3) give him the wrong initial concepts of reading." On the other hand, the "analytic or meaning method, starting with wholes, gives the child reinforcement of his learning not only from his success in the task itself, but also in the meaning gained from the short, attractive stories now available in increasing numbers for beginners." Strang cited no research backing her position.

The example Strang set for those perusing the *Reading Teacher* was anti-intellectual in a deeper way. Chall had noted, with puzzlement, that research findings rarely influence practical decisions about how to teach reading. Strang described this vice as a virtue: "The aim of these researches has been to arrive at generalizations, but the reading teacher and clinician deals with unique individuals. He is wise to make his decisions on the basis of his knowledge of the responses of the children whom he is teaching, rather than on generalizations which may or may not apply to the individual pupil."

This apology for the educational status quo either proves too little or too much. Doctors, like teachers, rely on generalizations while dealing with individuals. The research does not dictate how the doctor should treat each patient, but it does guide and limit that treatment. What responsible doctor would dismiss the clinical trial of a new drug out of hand, on the grounds that its findings might not apply to some individual patients?

Strang's review – undocumented and ill-argued in substance, hostile and dismissive in tone – was typical. Blanche Scheman, reviewing Chall's book in *Grade Teacher* (May/June 1968), insisted that the teacher, not the method of teaching, determines reading success. Eldonna Evertts, assistant executive secretary of the National Council of Teachers of English and a professor of elementary education at the University of Illinois, indicated by the awkwardness of her language in *Elementary English* the defensive crouch educators found themselves assuming: "Persons reading Dr. Chall's book will be startled by its bold and arrogant statements; few will feel comfortable while reading it. All will be challenged to seek explanations for its piercing statements. Some will engage in introspective analysis of their own cherished beliefs and half-hidden doubts."

But no one, least of all Evertts, suggested that the evidence Chall had marshaled might actually change anyone's mind. If those in the highest echelons of the education culture could so easily dismiss a meticulous literature review by a prestigious colleague – as they were still doing more than thirty years later (see http://coe.asu.edu/edrev/reviews/rev70.htm) – then how much hope could there be for research sponsored by a maverick textbook publisher?

SELLING WITH GUARANTEES

If evidence alone made few sales, maybe external inducements – guarantees based on evidence – would do better. As early as 1964, Open Court's promotional material boasted that many of its first-graders were "*writing* sentences and paragraphs that would be difficult, if not impossible, for first-graders to *read*, who have been taught by other methods." Blouke promised school personnel that if at any time before March 1965, "you are not completely satisfied, you may return everything except the workbooks, and owe us nothing except the return postage. . . . Why waste money on gadgets, when you can use this exciting, proven, inexpensive reading program?"

In 1969, the Nixon Administration enabled Open Court to hook its own promotion to a national crusade. Commissioner of Education James Allen, Jr., spoke to the National Association of State Boards of Education September 23, asserting that one out of four students nationwide had "significant reading deficiencies," and the adult population already included more than 3 million illiterates. Accordingly, "we should immediately set ourselves the goal of assuring that by the end of the 1970's the right to read shall be a reality to all." Speaking two months after the first manned moon landing, Allen described universal literacy as "education's 'moon' – the target for the decade ahead."

Literacy and illiteracy are notoriously plastic concepts, and Allen may have stretched them for dramatic effect. According to

Lawrence Stedman and Carl Kaestle, fewer than 1 million adults in 1979 rated themselves as illiterate. But Open Court's goal was to upgrade standards whatever the current situation might be, so Blouke responded enthusiastically. Within two months, in November 1969, the company issued a formal guarantee. Schools buying Open Court's first-grade textbooks would receive refunds if the books didn't produce the promised results –10 percent off per month of reading proficiency not gained, as shown on standardized tests of the school's choosing. Referring to Allen's call, Blouke announced that Open Court was "prepared to assume its share of the financial responsibility . . . in solving the current reading crisis in American schools."

The novelty of a guaranteed textbook sparked some newspaper stories, and in December 1969 it got Blouke a half-hour interview with assistant education commissioner Leon Lessinger and his assistant Albert Mayrhofer. "The interview was one of the most unusual ones I have ever had," Blouke wrote afterwards. "Somehow I could communicate with both of these gentlemen on a completely different level than with the normal educators. Subsequently I found out why: Dr. Lessinger is a biologist and Mr. Mayrhofer is some type of a scientist (I believe anthropologist.)."

Blouke expected guarantees to spread through the textbook industry. "Over a period of time, those who don't meet the claims of their guarantee are going to fall by the wayside," he told *Reading Newsreport* in April 1970. "As school boards increasingly demand publisher's accountability, those that hesitate to stand squarely behind their programs with legitimate guarantees will be conspicuous."

His expectations seemed reasonable at the time. Lessinger was calling for schools to adopt a "zero reject system." There was also a vogue for "performance contracting," in which a business would take over an entire school and guarantee results. The results of performance contracting were mixed; the response of professional educators was not. "It is pure myth that teachers can ever be held accountable, with justice, under current conditions," said National Education Association president Helen Bain. "The classroom teacher has either too little control or no control over the factors which might render accountability either feasible or fair." Another NEA official – evidently assuming that all business takeovers of schools would succeed – decried performance contracting because it tended to "discredit [public schools] in the eyes of the public." Their adamant refusal to be judged by results ultimately would doom Open Court's guarantee as well.

Blouke went beyond the guarantee in 1970–71, when he privately proposed that the federal government sponsor a competition among reading programs, which he believed Open Court would win. "The Federal Government alone is spending over $400,000,000 on reading-related programs," he wrote to David Keene of Vice-President Spiro Agnew's staff. "I believe the problem could be practically solved for less than $100,000,000," by using Open Court. "We believe our program can do the job better than any other publisher's because our method is broader and proven by experience, we can develop films to train masses of teachers, and the materials are inexpensive. I am convinced that if the Nixon Administration would take a *strong* position of leadership and *tell* the National Reading Center to *get the job moving this summer,* the result – teaching millions of unemployed how to read and write well enough to become employable – would be more significant politically and economically than the extremely dangerous and costly Family Assistance Plan." Even less plausibly, Blouke went on to assert, "If [Nixon] wanted to and is willing to make some difficult decisions, he could do the job before the next election in 1972."

In reality, Open Court was hard pressed to train the teachers it already had. General manager William Carroll told Blouke in 1973, "I shudder to think what the results will be if a school, new to Open Court, attempts to install our program in all grades simultaneously. I doubt that we could handle the teacher training problem adequately."

As we know now, around this time Nixon was making other difficult decisions, some of them criminal. But even in Commissioner Allen's initial 1969 speech, the administration had signaled that it would rather fail than challenge the education culture. First Allen asserted that a crash "right to read" program was feasible because of the "enormous amount of research and expertise in the field of reading" – and then he declared that expertise irrelevant. "We must avoid the danger of allowing education's reading 'moonshot' to become bogged down in debate over *methods* of the teaching of reading. It is the *goal* with which we must be concerned."

By the same process of reasoning, NASA in the 1960s would have devoted as much attention to catapults and slingshots as it had to rockets. In a tart post-mortem on the "right to read" program, CBE's Mortimer Smith used another metaphor. "If the cook's biscuits often fail to rise it is not sufficient to point out to her that edible biscuits are the goal," he wrote; "it becomes necessary to examine her method of preparation and baking. The lesson of recent years in reading instruction seems to be that redoubling your efforts and your expenditures without changing your methods is a poor road to reform."

The "right to read" program fell into bureaucratic oblivion. Some years later, Jeanne Chall reviewed National Assessment of Educational Progress results showing that it had indeed failed. "Less than 40 percent of all 17 year olds in 1984 scored on a level that permitted them to read and understand typical high school textbooks. Less than 20 per cent of the disadvantaged students were able to do so."

Open Court's greater willingness to challenge the education establishment did not save its guarantee from a similar oblivion. General manager Carroll recalls that the guarantee did succeed in "grabbing attention." And the program continued to produce the expected results. The company never had to pay a claim for non-performance, and in the fall of 1972 its guarantee was extended to second grade. But only a handful of small publishers, and no major ones, followed the company's lead. Any initial impact on Open Court sales did not last.

"Our salesmen tell us that the concept of a guarantee by a publisher is counter productive," Blouke eventually acknowledged. Teachers and supervisors were said to be "offended" or "frightened" by it. Their response is not as odd as it may seem. If textbooks were to be judged by results, could educators themselves be far behind? The very idea was alien to the education culture. Most educators were comfortable measuring accomplishment by the number of hours or days of school sessions, the number or percentage of students graduated, the number of courses offered – bureaucratic indicators of processes completed, not performance indicators of learning achieved.

Open Court's guarantee remained on the books as late as 1975, but it was rarely publicized. It was the most straightforward example in Open Court history of Blouke's initial engineering-style approach to changing the schools – don't argue, show results, and rake in the sales. But it barely rose to the level of failure. It came and went, leaving few traces in the sales charts or corporate folklore, because what appealed to engineers did not appeal to educators.

"Something is rotten in the heart of education," Blouke reflected, "if education is operated solely for the benefit of education." Evidently it would take more than information and promises to turn the culture around.

5. Trying to sell a principled program (1966–1973)

"Teaching new concepts to naive children is often as delicate a task as making an incision. Slight variations can make the difference between successful learning and discouraging confusion. This is not to say that there is only one way to present a concept, any more than there is only one way to perform a surgical operation. But it takes a very sophisticated practitioner to know which variations are optional and which are dangerous." – Carl Bereiter and Siegfried Engelmann, *Teaching Disadvantaged Children in the Preschool*

ECLECTIC WITH A PURPOSE

BLOUKE DREW ON sources as diverse as Nellie Thomas and Arther Trace to create the Open Court Correlated Language Arts Program. But the program itself was not a random collection of procedures that sounded good to him. Its parts worked together, so that the absence of any one made the rest less valuable; and they all worked toward the goal of making good literature accessible to children as early as possible. An Open Court teacher who ignored Workshop, for instance, would lose the opportunity to balance whole-class sessions and work with individuals or small groups. A teacher who failed to post wall-sound cards around the room would find it more difficult to teach phonics, and would then find the reading selections for the second half of first grade inaccessible to many students.

Few American elementary-school teachers are accustomed to proceeding in this way. They teach more or less as they were taught, mixing in appealing ideas from education school, from recent experiences, or from the "teacher's guide" that accompanied their textbooks, as they seem to be needed. Few teachers expect a textbook to prescribe a *system* of instruction. Thus Open Court's usual problem was not that it contradicted teachers' ideology, but that it violated their routine. As the University of Arizona's Virginia Richardson pointed out in a report on a staff development program in grades 4–6 published in *Educational Researcher* in 1990, "Changes that were adopted and tried out in the classroom were often dropped if they didn't 'work' for that teacher. . . . The rationale for an adopted research-based activity was seldom related to the original scholarly theory. For example, the rationale for asking students to read the comprehension check questions before reading a passage was consistently expressed as making sure the students got the right answers and did better on the tests, rather than the theoretical rationale derived from schema theory." (See Chapter 8.)

The fact that most teachers didn't have a system and weren't looking for one did away with Blouke's original hope that Open Court would be an "idiot-proof" program. As early as November 1964, sales manager Randall Kratz reported that the company's new customers needed help. "We found teachers who were actually afraid to start the program on their own, others who used the method incorrectly, and still others who needed a little encouragement and someone to tell them that what they were doing was correct." As Open Court adapted to this reality, it began to shed the arrogant and naive belief that University of Arizona political scientist Sheila Tobias finds underlying many educational reforms – the belief that "once articulated, the 'right way' will be self-evident, teacher-proof, and that it will not need to be hammered home or to be translated into incremental steps."

To translate its big ideas into incremental steps Open Court had available two tools: a dedicated corps of "consultants," usually former Open Court teachers, employed to train new teachers in how to use the program; and written teacher guides that accompanied the textbooks at each level. Each had its own virtues and defects. Consultants could and did creatively adapt their presentations to their audiences, and they were hard to ignore – but their message might vary from what the home office wanted, and teachers might not retain it all. Written teachers' guides, on the other hand, were durable and presumably always "on message" (being written in the home office) – but would the teachers read and understand them?

CONSULTANTS AND SALES

"In the southeast," recalls Karen Hansill, "if we could get Open Court in the public schools classroom by classroom, usually starting with first grade, it would work. The process was very slow and very labor-intensive." Who could do the labor? As soon as Blouke began hiring consultants and salespeople and editors in 1964, he faced much the same dilemma as the education establishment had faced earlier in the 20th century – a sudden need for a kind of personnel of which there was no adequate supply.

Nothing could substitute for a professional sales force of flesh-and-blood people to visit, make contacts, explain, and sell. But they couldn't be just any people. Experienced Open Court teachers often made good proselytizers, but there weren't enough of them. Professional salespeople, on the other hand, had worked for other textbook companies and were accustomed to catering to the existing educational market, not trying to change it. They had trouble representing Open Court because they didn't understand it. No wonder Blouke reflected, after the company was sold in 1996, that the hardest part of running it had been hiring the right people.

Technically, Open Court consultants and salespeople had different roles. In practice the work and the personnel often overlapped. Convincing a teacher or a district to try Open Court in the first place was an educational process in itself, which post-adoption training just continued. When things got out of hand, consultants could take corrective action, as Nellie Thomas herself did when she visited the Mt. Healthy school district in Ohio in September 1966. She found she had to do "a terrific amount of work," because "Mt. Healthy children are being subjected to the same old language practices with a *veneer* of my program." It wouldn't be the last time.

Over time, those working "in the field" created an oral Open Court tradition. They shared the Caruses' general view that schools could do better. And they conveyed to rank-and-file teachers the crucial idea that Open Court was a principled program in which each element depended to some degree on every other. Their work may have built on the company's published guides, but that left plenty of room for variations. As early as 1972 Blouke complained about "gross inconsistencies between our teachers' guides . . . and what our consultants recommend at teacher training workshops." The gap was never quite bridged.

Consultants soon realized, for instance, that while repetition was necessary for kids to get comfortable with written language, there was no need for it to be boring. As lead consultant Jerry Lebo reported in 1972, "We've worked out five different ways to review wall sound cards. We've worked out seven different ways to do sentence lifting. Ten different ways to do Words to Watch. A dozen different ways to do spelling activities."

Open Court's oral tradition was conservative as well as creative, if only because any significant change in the company's programs threatened the existing group of satisfied customers. Administrative assistant Beth Niejwik recalls that in the mid-1990s "there seemed to be a tendency in the field to want to make *CYS* [the new program] sound like a prettier, more user-friendly version of *OCRW* [the old program]. That way, the customer who was happy with *OCRW* would feel reassured that *CYS* would have all the same benefits, would work the same way, but would just be easier to use." But the same conservatism that often led salespeople to lobby for stasis or a less demanding program also enabled them to resist when mistakes came from the top of the company, as in 1985 (chapter 9).

Even at the first-grade level, a basic discrepancy persisted between the company's written and oral cultures, André Carus recalls. Blouke and top authors "saw the importance of teaching the concept [of sound-symbol correspondence] and then quickly moving into real reading. The field tended to want more practice on each individual correspondence first."

The field force often relayed customer complaints that Open Court's readers were too difficult. Speaking to salesmen and consultants in 1973, Blouke insisted, "I still think that the vocabulary level and level of sophistication is about right," and hoped that, once the books had been revised and training improved, "Our customers will find the stories just about right, too."

More seriously for Blouke's long-term goals, the oral culture of the company concentrated on beginning reading and phonics and had little to say about literature and liberal education. It was understandable that Lebo and other consultants did so; the first task was difficult enough. Many teachers had neither learned nor taught phonics before. Others had done so only in the off-and-on way suggested by the major basals, where letter sounds were taught as an afterthought, often only on a "discovery" basis, and often using only beginning and ending sounds.

TEACHERS' GUIDES

Consultants and sales staff weren't always the company's ideal messengers. But Open Court's printed teachers' guides were problematic in different ways throughout the company's history, for several reasons:

* Teachers expected a teacher's guide to provide a summary of the day's story and a number of ideas for teaching it. They did not expect to have to learn a new set of teaching techniques from it. If the company chose to describe a new teaching technique in full in the guide, it risked inducing panic if a teacher opened the book the night before class. If the company instead relegated teaching techniques to a special handbook or a set of special cards, they might well gather dust.

* Over time the guides diverged from what consultants were saying. In 1984, André Carus was still hoping to get in writing "some of the striking and memorable things about the program that our consultants say at presentations, but which have somehow never found their way into the guides." Sometimes they did. The teacher's introduction to *Headway* (1979) echoed Lebo's thoughts when it urged teachers to "jump into action quickly. Avoid rambling introductions and pointless questioning of the 'Does anyone know what a sentence is?' kind." But there was never enough.

* They weren't easy to use. In 1973, Open Court consultant Angela Flannigan protested, "I spend too much of my time . . . trying to soothe and/or win over frustrated, angry teachers who find the guides do not give them the help they need," especially in grades 2–6. Even later on, "They were not cross-referenced well," says veteran salesperson Karen Hansill. "They had a lot of loose components, they never had decent indexes. . . . We *never* handed out the teachers' guides for [prospective customers] to look at. We had to sell teachers first on the philosophy and how it was good for students and that we would be there to help. We'd show them the student books, but the teachers' guides were the kiss of death."

From the beginning the company sold best in grade one, despite repeated attempts to broaden sales into later grades, in part because the first-grade teachers' guides were easier to follow. "This is my 29th year of teaching," Anastasia Kenney of Blue River, Wisconsin, wrote to Nellie Thomas in 1966, and [I] can sincerely say that I have *never* had such results! All but two of my first graders are reading *Weekly Reader* and read library books, newspaper captions and primary magazines fluently. I wish you could hear them!"

But Kenney and her colleagues had no way to tell which ingredients were critical to producing good results and which were incidental. Many wanted to know, because they felt there weren't enough hours in the day or weeks in the year to do everything the program recommended. What should their priorities be? Blending? Wall sound cards? Fast-paced teaching? Using a dozen different spelling drills? Should the teacher put more energy and time into working with students in whole-class settings? Or in the flexible groups that Workshop made possible?

Even within the company disagreements on priorities remained, and little research was available to help resolve them. As a result, teachers never knew which corners they could safely cut. Converts often became dogmatists, and Open Court – somewhere along the way skeptics began calling it "Open Cult" – was seen as more monolithic and systematic, and even harder to understand, than it needed to be.

EVANGELISM

With all these layers of confusion and uncertainty and cross-pur-
poses, one might wonder how Open Court succeeded as well as it
did. As luck would have it, Nellie Thomas had already provided a
key when Blouke found her stumping the Midwest, making teachers cry as she railed against publishers for wasting money on worksheets. A quasi-religious conversion experience was not something Blouke was equipped to provide, but he recognized its
value.

Among Thomas's early converts was Jerry Lebo, a Hettinger,
North Dakota, teacher and president of the North Dakota
Council of Language Arts. Lebo began using Open Court materials in his classroom in 1964–65 and went to work for the company in August 1966. In the late 1960s, Lebo and two other consultants barnstormed the country to drum up business. They would
choose a location – usually on the edge of a large population center so as to be accessible to small communities as well – rent a
hotel room, send out invitations, and conduct one workshop in
the afternoon and another in the evening. Then they would pack
up and move to the next location, doing the same thing the next
day. Over the next three decades, Lebo shaped the company's
image more than any individual other than the Caruses.

"I've seen more classrooms and more teachers and more
schools than any living individual in this country," Lebo told a
company seminar in the spring of 1972. "The most significant
thing I have seen . . . is the lack of any significant teaching act of
any kind." He said the same thing to teachers – convincing them
of their sinful sloth, offering redemption by Open Court, and
then training them in its use. Perhaps the company could have
managed without Lebo's unique set of talents, but his approach
made a big difference.

In 1972, Lebo opined that Open Court's Foundation Program
succeeded "because it forces teaching. You cannot sit on your butt
behind the desk. If you do, the program doesn't work. You've got
to get up out of the desk, on the floor, move with the kids, keep it
alive and active and you start to see results. The minute you go sit
behind your desk, it doesn't work."

But even Lebo's rhetorical skills could not always move his audience. "I pound away at [first-grade teachers] that you stand in front of the class and you tell them what to do and then you do it with them so that that page is done in about three minutes." Instead, "I find teachers that take forty-five minutes per dictation simply because they don't understand how to dialogue with the class."

In an article published in the April 1990 issue of *Exceptional Children*, researchers Janice Baker and Naomi Zigmond confirm Lebo's description of the education-culture inertia that he was pushing against, even in a school that used Open Court:

"The teachers did not seem insensitive to the needs of the slowest or the fastest student; but they were more committed to routine than to addressing individual differences. . . . Furthermore, although a majority of teachers' time was devoted to instructional activities, very little time was spent teaching. Classes were quiet and controlled in large part because worksheets and workbooks were standard fare. . . . Although students were attentive and seemed to be doing what they were told, there was no feeling of intensity or urgency in the learning that was taking place."

Along with speed, Lebo advocated proximity. "Most of what you do with the whole class should be done with most of the kids in that class within touching distance. . . . I should be able to reach out and touch you from where I'm working."

Why get close? he was asked. "I taught high school," he replied. "I've seen those kids, 70% in many classes, who all through eleven grades, before they got to be seniors sat in the back desk in the corner. They took their D and they were glad to get it. And the teacher was glad to give it to them. They got through eleven years of school without doing anything. Without being taught anything. And one of the ways to get at those kids is to get them up where they can see and hear and get them up where they almost have to get involved." Through serendipity and good judgment, Open Court was aimed at the heart as well as the head.

6. Gaining credibility (1968–1974)

"In the past fifty years American educational theory has become almost entirely isolated from the tradition of European education. There are many reasons for this phenomenon, but one of them is the little known but vital fact that for the past thirty or forty years our leading pedagogues in America have held Ed.D. (Doctor of Education) degrees rather than Ph.D. (Doctor of Philosophy) degrees. One of the multitude of differences between the two degrees is that the holder of the Ed.D. degree is spared the inconvenience of learning any foreign language. (The Ph.D. candidate is examined in at least two foreign languages.)" – Arther Trace, Jr., *Reading without Dick & Jane*, 1965

GETTING ADVICE

HAVING A PROGRAM that got results in the classroom was not enough. Open Court also needed the credibility that came from being endorsed by well-known and respected professionals. Most textbook companies obtained this by hiring "authors" who contributed little to the operation beyond their names and an occasional speech at professional meetings. Open Court was neither willing nor financially able to go this route, and few professional educators would have been willing to endorse the company's approach in any case. But in July 1968 Blouke announced an analogous scheme. He would form an Editorial Advisory Board of members "distinguished by significant contributions in the field of education and letters." They would not be authors, but they would "assist in guiding" the textbook program and "review current materials and long-range plans."

Blouke gives credit to then-general manager Bill Carroll for being willing to invest in recruiting such a board and holding annual meetings. "He thought it would be a better promotion than advertising." Already the following month, editor Sherwood Sugden wanted the field-test edition of the company's remedial-reading program to include the names of any board members already selected.

That fall Blouke and Marianne visited a number of potential advisory-board members on the West Coast, among them Arthur Bestor, Frances Clarke Sayers, and Berkeley assistant dean of education and California Curriculum Commissioner James Jarrett. The results were mixed. Bestor had become much less active in curriculum reform than in the 1950s. Sayers was sympathetic but unable to travel.

Blouke's uncomfortable meeting with Jarrett epitomized his antipathy to the education culture as a whole. Jarrett talked about three revolutions in American education – progressive education, the Bestor revolution, and the then-current equality revolution – and left Blouke unimpressed. "When I asked him about these various revolutions, he did not seem to have much judgment. For example, his only comment about the Bestor revolution was that it was 'kaput,' and he pronounced this badly; he pronounced it 'kupoot.' This word doesn't mean anything except to indicate an emotional reaction." Blouke considered their meeting "quite unsatisfactory" and dismissed any thought of inviting Jarrett to join the advisory board. "After all we have sent him and talked to him, especially during the [1967] California adoption, he never visited an Open Court classroom or talked to an Open Court teacher."

The sixteen invited Editorial Advisory Board members who did gather at La Salle in June 1969 included:

* Jacques Barzun of Columbia University, described as "one of the principal contemporary defenders of the grand tradition of Western humanism";
* Carl Bereiter, a cognitive psychologist at the Ontario Institute for Studies in Education;
* Clifton Fadiman, author, editor, and media personality;
* Louise Gurren, NYU speech professor and Open Court consultant;

* Clifton Hall, Tennessee education professor;
* Jeffrey Hart, Dartmouth English professor;
* Russell Kirk, conservative luminary;
* James Koerner, who had edited *The Case for Basic Education;*
* John Latimer, George Washington University classicist;
* Sterling McMurrin, University of Utah philosopher;
* Edwin Moldof, Great Books Foundation academic director;
* William Robinson, Rhode Island education commissioner;
* Arther Trace, Open Court author;
* William Viall, Western Michigan University education professor and executive secretary of the National Association of State Directors of Teacher Education and Certification;
* Ruth Hill Viguers, author and Simmons College children's literature expert; and
* Rolf Weil, president of Roosevelt University in Chicago.

Substantially the same group met again each year until 1973 and once more in 1978. "We were looking for a diversity of background," recalls Blouke. Nevertheless, CBE members and supporters predominated.

Open Court published the proceedings of four of the board's six meetings under the title *Papers on Educational Reform.* Many of these papers were general to the point of being academic. They ranged widely in tone, including the boilerplate (Sidney Hook lamenting "the disorder of our times" in 1974), the incisive (Kenneth Clark noting in 1971 that one burden of a majority-minority school was that "you have no way of protecting yourself from innovative programs"), the scholarly (Barzun contending that educational folly came not from Romanticism but from unintelligent application of principles), and the pathetic (Latimer touting a classics curriculum that featured Superlegatus, "a *Superman* figure, who becomes involved in a series of exciting adventures").

Many of the board's discussions were abstract, in part because Blouke expected the group to explore what liberal education could be, as a kind of vanishing point or ultimate objective toward which Open Court might strive. The board also proved to be a seedbed for new initiatives. Some became saleable Open Court textbooks (kindergarten, math), some did not (music, grammar). Others fit in with Blouke's overall educational goals. At the June 1972 meeting in Lake Bluff, Illinois, A. D. C. Peterson introduced the fledgling International Baccalaureate, a secondary-level program involving "a combination of general liberal arts education with a sufficient degree of specialisation" which corresponded "very closely to the recommendations in Admiral Rickover's paper on 'A National Scholastic Standard,'" which has since become prominent on the American educational-reform scene. Conversations among the Caruses, Fadiman, and Viguers led to the 1973 founding of the widely acclaimed *Cricket* magazine, which has since spawned numerous offspring, still published by the family firm.

As planned, the Editorial Advisory Board gave the company a sounding board and some impressive names to put inside the front cover of its readers. "It gave us some authority," Blouke said later. But as time passed, the company's authority increasingly came not from high-profile endorsers, but from Open Court's alignment with the results starting to emerge from high-quality educational research, detailed in Chapter 8.

By the spring of 1975, the company was short of funds and short of time – in part due to the projects germinated at Educational Advisory Board gatherings. Blouke regretfully canceled the board's 1975 meeting. In the meantime, one of its members had gone from reviewing plans to becoming an author of Open Court programs.

CARL BEREITER IN THE PRESCHOOL

Unlike any other member of the Editorial Advisory Board, Carl Bereiter had spent time with radical reformers anathema to the Council for Basic Education, like Ivan Illich and John Holt. A generation younger than many of the board's other members and a cognitive psychologist, he was more interested in investigating the process of learning than in pronouncing on it. His continued presence and influence on the company were a signal that Blouke could attract people to carry his original idea beyond his own reach.

"I look back with some nostalgia to the days when all I bothered to think about was what seemed to be the best way of educating children," Bereiter told the board in May 1970. Being the best had been the cornerstone of Blouke's strategy too, but it was not enough. As one of the authors of the company's new kindergarten program, Bereiter found himself trying to devise a program "that would not only be good educationally but that would also be acceptable so that it would, in fact, be used."

Bereiter had personal experience with unacceptability. In the middle 1960s, he and Siegfried Engelmann, then both at the University of Illinois, had conceived and initiated a preschool for fifteen four-and-a-half-year olds who were considered to be, as we now say, "at risk" because of family background and low scores on standard language tests. (The two have long since gone their separate ways, but this early collaboration still leads some to confuse their later work.)

The preschool's program involved direct instruction in subjects that the children would need in order to keep up in school. "From the first day," Bereiter and Engelmann wrote, "the children were given an intensive, fast-paced, highly structured program of instruction in basic language skills, reading, and arithmetic. Each of these three subjects was taught as a separate class, each with its own teacher, the children circulating in groups of five from class to class. Classes were 15 minutes in length, expanding to 20 minutes as the children became better adjusted to the routine. The only other major educational activity was singing, where specially written songs were employed to give additional practice in skills being taught in the classes."

The children made rapid progress. After ten weeks, "they had begun to use well-articulated sentences and to talk *about* things, rather than merely using language to express wants and feelings. By that time, too, the children had progressed from not knowing how to count past five to being able to solve simple equations involving addition and subtraction, and from not being able to tell whether two printed characters were alike or different to being able to sound out a few three-letter words." After seven months, many of the children – who had yet to attend kindergarten – seemed ready for first-grade reading and arithmetic.

Observers' responses to the children changed accordingly. Early on, visitors were impressed that these "culturally deprived" preschoolers could count and recognize letters of the alphabet. "Later, when the children were struggling with reading and arithmetic, visitors seemed to be less and less impressed, not because of what the children were doing but because the visitors seemed now to perceive the children as average children who were having a tough time. Finally, as the children became proficient in basic skills and went on to master tasks well beyond their years, visitors began reacting to them as if they were culturally privileged, academically talented children and began raising questions as to where this would all lead, how we would help the children develop their creative abilities, and so on."

Such a systematic and unsentimental effort to prevent schools from reproducing social inequalities was even more unusual then than now. Bereiter and Engelmann chronicled the experiment and explained its rationale in *Teaching Disadvantaged Children in the Preschool*, published by Prentice-Hall in 1966.

Most preschools for the disadvantaged, they wrote, had been modeled after preschools for upper-middle-class children. Such children already had the necessary verbal and intellectual skills for school, and typically benefited from a more permissive, sociable, and active milieu than that offered in their own homes. "In complementing or offsetting the upper-middle-class home environment, the nursery school has taken on many of the characteristics of the lower-class home environment," they wrote.

That was fine – for upper-middle-class kids. "But it is ridiculous to call the experiences provided by such a school compensatory when they are administered to children from lower-class backgrounds." Those children needed what *they* weren't getting at home. Since they typically started out a year behind the average and fell farther behind as they moved through school, their preschool education had to give priority to academic objectives. This line of thought, Bereiter and Engelmann concluded, should "encourage the serious and open-minded educator to consider entirely new approaches which are truly compensatory and which focus directly upon the crucial problems of disadvantaged children."

This was hardly the kind of class analysis fashionable in the 1960s. A characteristic response came from Jeanette Veatch of the University of Southern California, in an April 1968 talk published in the September issue of *Childhood Education*. Veatch questioned "why achievement is so overridingly important in a society that has killed two of its major leaders, that is involved in a shooting war, that is in the process of burning down its cities, and that still has no legislation to prevent the sale of firearms." She condemned Bereiter and Engelmann for "behaviorism" and "cold lack of humanitarian values" because they believed that learning sometimes had to be instilled "from the outside in." Instead, Veatch insisted, "Learning must come from the inside out. . . . Sight vocabulary must be taught as Sylvia Ashton-Warner describes. . . . We must help each child find himself." The possibility that such instruction would leave disadvantaged children floundering academically went unmentioned.

INSINUATING STRUCTURE INTO KINDERGARTEN

As this response indicates, by 1969 Bereiter had already made himself anathema to the education culture. So it was only natural that Blouke should recruit him, first for the Editorial Advisory Board, and then to review and ultimately help Ann Hughes write Open Court's kindergarten program. Following the lead of Bereiter's own preschool and of other Open Court programs, its daily teaching menu included one-and-one-half hours of language development, counting and measuring, conceptual development, perceptual games and activities, social development and self-awareness, and music.

Open Court faced the prospect of selling this relatively structured program to teachers and administrators, many of whom (as Bereiter told the Editorial Advisory Board) "consider structure – or deliberate teaching of any kind – harmful and having no place in the lives of young children." Instead, they believe that "life adjustment – teaching of attitudes, values, and social behaviors – is the most important thing for the kindergarten to accomplish. . . . The teaching of skills, in and of itself, is generally regarded as a good thing, but on the other hand, rote learning, drill, practice are considered bad things. . . . Teaching thinking is [considered] a good thing, but correcting children and letting them know that something they've said doesn't make sense is a bad thing."

No wonder Open Court programs could not be sold simply on results. The very concept of "results" in the education culture was confused, approving a goal but disdaining the means that might achieve it.

Bereiter concluded that "Many of the concerns of childhood educators can be either allayed or aggravated simply by the way in which you present what you're doing." He and Engelmann had managed to alarm them. Others, he saw, "simply hooked [the same approach] up to a different set of ideas – or to a different set of slogans, to be more precise." So when Bereiter came to write the introduction to Open Court's kindergarten program, he did not repeat the preschool book's stern call for open-minded educators to change their minds about everything.

"At the very least," the introduction begins, "a Kindergarten program should insure that what children learn in Kindergarten is more valuable than what they would learn if they stayed home. All Kindergarten programs consist of wholesome, enjoyable activities that promote learning of some kind, but in many activities it is difficult to discover just what is being learned and to judge whether it is more valuable than the learning that all children acquire, whether they go to Kindergarten or not. In designing the Open Court Kindergarten Program we began by recognizing that most of what young children learn is not learned in school, so that a school program cannot be considered in isolation, but must be considered in the light of what it adds to the enormous and valuable experience of home and neighborhood. Accordingly, we have not designed a program that replaces the natural experience of childhood but one that supplements it, by contributing those special kinds of learning that a wise teacher is best able to supply."

This masterful rhetoric uses the teacher's sense of professional worth as a lever to turn Dewey's argument for experiential education upside down. If we're going to have kindergarten at all – and since most readers of the introduction were already employed in kindergartens, they weren't likely to challenge that! – then why should it merely repeat kids' normal experience and omit the contributions of a "wise teacher"?

Bereiter's introduction goes on to urge that "in order to acquire a love of learning, [the child] must recognize that learning exists." Such recognition would be "a difficult thing for the child to acquire if all his learning is casual and unstructured." And so, "In the Open Court Kindergarten Program we have tried to make learning visible and definite enough that the child knows learning is going on – he can see the results from day to day – and even develop some understanding of how it goes on. We believe that the love of learning, as with any other kind of love, if it is to last, should not be blind."

Did you notice the insinuation of "structure"? No one for whom child-centered education was a set of ideas, as opposed to a set of slogans, would be fooled by this, but Open Court wasn't trying to sell books to them.

7. Math: forward to thinking, not back to basics (1971–1984)

"Children should be placed in activity situations in which they must solve (individually or by group discussion) some real problem. This activity and game approach is different from some 'open classroom' proposals in that each activity has a very specific purpose and the children are generally told what activity is appropriate for them." – Stephen Willoughby, April 1975

AMBITION

OPEN COURT SOUGHT to teach reading and writing so well that the entire American curriculum would have to be upgraded. But the company's ambition soon rose beyond that. Blouke wanted to do more than just make upgrading possible, he wanted to participate in it.

Of course this was not the only possible strategy. General manager William Carroll recalls arguing that the company should focus on its strength in phonics. He didn't think Open Court could be as distinctive or as competitive against the big firms in the higher grades as it was in first grade. Besides, "If you teach kids to read, you never have to do another right thing in your life."

Carroll did not win that argument, and in the late 1960s and early 1970s, the company embarked on an ambitious plan, sinking considerable time and money into developing textbooks for elementary math, science, and music. In the end, only mathematics made it to publication, because it had the biggest potential market, and because Open Court lacked the resources to compete in all fields.

Indeed, math and reading and writing may have been the

only subjects where Open Court's academic ambitions stood a chance. "No matter how misguided educators may be in how they go about teaching reading and math," Carl Bereiter wrote at the time, "there is no question that they are serious about it and are thus potentially reachable by a program that demonstrates results." In contrast, "no such long-range hope can be entertained for the potential market of a science program. It could prove results and still be rejected because it was too much bother."

That was true for music, as the principal of a model Open Court school in Connecticut told Blouke's sister Theo Carus in April 1972. "I decided to try to talk Mr. Fabri into using our second grade music program" then under development, she reported. "Since the school is sold on Open Court and Mr. Fabri is a professional week-end musician, it shouldn't have been a problem. Mr. Fabri said, 'One hundred plus minutes a week on music? Revolutionary. I didn't start music until I was in fifth grade.' He used the word revolutionary at least four times; and he turned me down flat."

TO BECOME A NATIVE SPEAKER OF MATHEMATICS

As he had in reading, Blouke began the Open Court mathematics and science program by seeking out the best people in the field. In the late 1960s and early 1970s, he and his brother Paul met with a series of experts, among them future *Real Math* authors Joe Rubinstein and Peter Hilton. They hoped to develop a program that would highlight the close relationship between math and science.

Meanwhile mathematics had also caught the attention of Carl Bereiter and Ann Hughes in Toronto. They had been trying to teach thinking skills to a group of sixteen above-average seventh-graders, but the students' math deficiencies kept intruding. In a key 1971 essay distributed by Open Court ("Does Mathematics Have to Be So Awful?"), Bereiter reflected on this experience.

The seventh graders, he found, could be quick and inventive when faced with mathematical situations. But when a problem resembled one they had already encountered in their math books, they froze. Paradoxically, instruction seemed to have moved them backwards. Bereiter began to appreciate why most elementary-school teachers dislike math. "It is no fun teaching something that breeds stupidity, where you can see your pupils getting dumber and dumber as the year goes by."

At this time there were two main approaches to teaching basic mathematics – either rote drill ("old math," soon to be reincarnated as "back to basics"), or early explanation of sophisticated concepts ("new math"). Neither approach fostered mathematical literacy. Of course, as in the case of look-say reading, students found ways to get by. One Toronto math consultant told Ann Hughes that when she was herself faced with a problem such as subtracting 29 from 47, she began by saying mentally, "9 from 7, you can't do it; 9 from 17 is 8," and so on – a makeshift that made Hughes irate at the way the consultant had learned arithmetic. "*This* babyism, continued through 20 years of professional life, is a real atrocity."

Bereiter compared learning math to learning a foreign language, implying that both old and new math were misconceived. One might "learn" a foreign language by rote, old-math style, and end up like the tourist who parrots a few phrases from a book and understands replies only if they follow the same stereotyped pattern. Alternatively, one might "learn" a foreign language new-math style, by studying its grammar, syntax, and etymology, but be unable to carry on a simple conversation in it.

But neither the tourist nor the linguist learns to use the language as a native-born speaker can. "When is it proper to say 'I like the skiing' rather than 'I like skiing'?" wrote Bereiter. "An enormously complicated array of conditions bears upon the use of the definite article in English, making it one of the most difficult points of the language for foreigners to learn. Yet native speakers of English have acquired such consistency of usage that the matter is not taught in school, is not even recognized as an issue, and it is the rare person who has even given a moment's thought to how he decides when to say 'the' and when not."

It is that *functional* understanding that we also seek in mathematics. Children don't need to begin by memorizing definitions of counting, addition, subtraction, or place value. Instead they need a familiarization process, a systematic "messing around" with numbers, that will provide them with the same everyday ability to count, add, subtract, recognize place value, and more that they already have with verb tenses and use of the definite article. Bereiter described a simple place-value game by way of example. "Children toss coins at a target, which is in the form of a four-digit numeral – say 1 3 2 4. The score for a toss is determined by the digit the child's coin comes closest to, but place value is honored. Thus landing on the 4 is worth just four points but landing on the 2 is worth two tens or twenty points. . . . The goal of all this is simple. By the end of the phase, the child should never look at a digit in a numeral without thinking of what place it's in and he should have complete facility in making exchanges between one place and another."

Learning the definition of "commutative" (new math) or reciting the multiplication tables (old math) might seem more intellectual, more "educational," than playing this game. But they're not. Here again, Open Court, regardless of the political rhetoric about education, found itself using non-traditional techniques in the service of traditional intellectual goals.

The insight that children can learn to speak and write mathematics without becoming mathematicians, just as they learn to speak English without becoming linguists, should have been good news for schools. Elementary math may always be taught by generalists who dislike the subject and do not understand it well themselves. But they can still teach it successfully. A well-considered sequence of self-checking games and activities can enable students to use math concepts that neither they nor their teacher may be able to (or need to) verbalize fully.

This option is rarely available in teaching science. Teachers would have to understand the subject matter, and this was not likely to happen – as was vividly illustrated when the authors of Open Court's fledgling science program reviewed some science materials in 1973 and agreed that it would be necessary to caution elementary teachers against equating "gas" [matter neither solid nor liquid] with "gasoline" [the petroleum product]. After a few years the science program fell by the wayside. As Hughes put it,

Open Court did not seek merely to produce programs with which good teachers could teach able children from good backgrounds. It wanted to produce materials that would be accessible "to low-ability children from poor backgrounds, taught by mediocre teachers."

BOOK LEARNING

No teacher could enjoy seeing students incuriously accept a sum smaller than any of its addends. Yet math classes often produce just such incompetence. "It is not perversity on the part of teachers that this is so," Bereiter wrote. "When the preferred goal is poorly defined and there is no available way to teach it, there is a natural tendency to teach something more-or-less related, where the goals are clearer and means are available." (And the absence of the needed knowledge is not the fault of the rank-and-file teaching corps.) This adaptive response is a key part of the culture of American education regardless of subject matter.

"Teachers generally spent very little time presenting new material or helping students *understand* material previously taught," Thomas Good of the University of Missouri-Columbia told a special interest session of the American Educational Research Association in 1984. He had observed fifty-six math lessons in thirty-seven fourth-, fifth-, and sixth-grade classrooms in nine schools.

"Many teachers emphasized the mechanics of an operation," he wrote, "as opposed to explaining basic concepts and how and why procedures work. The focus was on memorization rather than on understanding and visualizing concepts and making generalizations. For example, in explaining division problems such as 38 divided by 9, one teacher stressed the steps used in dividing rather than providing students with concrete materials with which to practice dividing. . . . References to everyday situations were infrequent, and pictures in the text were often the only examples used. The attention given to meaning varied from classroom to classroom, but in general the teaching we observed emphasized procedural detail instead of understanding." The much larger Third International Math and Science Study, ably summarized in

Stigler and Hiebert's *The Teaching Gap*, confirms Good's dismal findings.

Actually Good was describing a relatively favorable case. Math classes also breed stupidity by being designed so that students can avoid learning outright. "Children seldom find it necessary to read [word] problems or think about them," wrote Steve Willoughby, who succeeded Hughes, after her unexpected and premature death in 1972, as principal author of the Open Court math program. "They discover – or in some cases are actually taught – techniques for getting the right answer without having read the problems or understood what is being asked." He described three:

* Look for "key words" like "left," which is taken to mean that the smaller of two numbers mentioned should be subtracted from the larger.
* Discover that all the word problems on a given page require the same operation. "When she was in third grade, my daughter arrived home one day with a sheet of word problems. She worked for about three minutes and then asked me how to do the first. After quick examination I established that this was the easiest problem on the page, so I suggested that we do one of the harder problems, assuming she would then be able to figure out how to do the easier problems. Wendy looked at me, a slight air of disdain creeping into her voice. 'Daddy,' she said patiently, 'if I know how to do the first problem, I'll know how to do them all.'"
* Apply a more sophisticated rule of thumb: "If there are more than two numbers in the problem, you add. If there are two big numbers, you subtract. If there's a small number and a big number, you divide, and if it doesn't come out even (whole number), you multiply. If there are two small numbers, you multiply."

As Open Court editor Tom Anderson had once said, among students and teachers, the primary conspiracy is not to teach and not to learn.

REAL MATH: FIELD TESTING AND FEEDBACK

Real Math, as general manager Howard Webber christened it, underwent by far the longest and most thorough field testing of any Open Court program. It was written one year at a time, then rewritten the following summer in view of the preceding year's teaching experience. After a few years of preparation, the first-grade program was tried out in 1973–74. "We worked closely with our field-test teachers," wrote Joe Rubinstein; "we visited class-rooms, we taught our own lessons, and we conducted teacher-training workshops. We received lesson-by-lesson written evaluations from all of our field-test teachers." Using this feedback, the authors revised the first-grade program and wrote a second-grade program, and then field-tested the first-grade program for the second time and the second-grade program for the first time, and so on. They came to appreciate what Blouke referred to as the Willoughby Principle: "No matter how certain we were that an idea would work in the classroom, we always learned something from field testing. As a rule, less than 50 percent of the first version of any particular grade level of Real Math made it into the second year of the field test."

Keeping field tests going required Rubinstein to recruit a new group of teachers every year at each school. "If the teachers in the lower grades of the school liked the program, which virtually all of them did, there was some pressure on the teachers in the next grade to go along with us. . . . in one of our successful field test sites in Broadview, Illinois, we established an excellent working relationship with the 1st grade teachers; in fact, we learned an awful lot from them. And the same is true for the 2nd grade teachers and the 3rd grade teachers. The children were doing well in arithmetic, the teachers loved the program, and, in fact, they were enthusiastic. They sounded like Open Court salesmen." Then disaster struck. "The 4th grade teachers would simply not go along with the field testing. I wrote them letters; I offered to give them the books and let them use their own books as well, and just select activities because we wanted to follow what these children were doing after they left 3rd grade and went into 4th grade.

The teachers wouldn't even answer my letters. They were simply not interested." And that was the end of that field test.

By 1978, when the K-2 editions first became publicly available, the company was giving the fifth-grade program its first field test, while the first-grade program was getting its fifth. That year the field tests involved 5600 children and 238 teachers in 21 states. Senior author Stephen Willoughby taught *Real Math* once a week at St. John the Baptist School in Yonkers, New York, and followed a class from grade one through grade six, "graduating" with them in 1979.

"Impeccable," said Thomas Nelson & Sons when it considered (and declined) the program for possible Canadian sale. "I've never heard of a series with a comparable field-test history." As important as the field tests' duration was the authors' ability to respond to teachers' concerns without compromising the program's principles. When first-grade teachers complained that the draft program didn't give kids enough practice in writing numerals, Rubinstein acknowledged that they were right. But "rather than blindly following the dictates of the teachers and include more pages of numeral writing, which would have meant that other pages had to come out of the book, we carefully went back, rethought the problems, and came up with a game: the tracing and writing numerals game, which finally appeared in the 3rd edition of first grade. The game gives the children lots of practice with writing numerals. They can use it over and over and over again and it takes up only one page of the workbook. Not only that, instead of wasting all that time on just learning to write numerals, the game helps children with numerical sequence. . . . So we didn't just blindly say, well let's write more pages for numeral writing. We went back and rethought how we could do that and do other things at the same time."

Like the reading program before it, Open Court's math program had its idiosyncrasies. It depended to an unusual extent on games and on students working together in pairs. Students responded to the teacher's questions by displaying "response cubes." Proper use of the cubes, Hughes wrote, "requires intensive training by the teacher over a period of several days." This and other idiosyncrasies could create problems for students who transferred in during the year or even between school years, or began the program after first grade. Jerry Lebo acknowledged that "Grades K, 1, and 4 are the best pilots for us, because we always get into catch-up problems with 2-3 and 5-6."

NOT BACK TO BASICS

The math authors shared a seemingly obvious goal – "preparing the child to use mathematics in his or her life," as Peter Hilton put it. To do so they aimed to teach certain basic skills, enumerated by Joe Rubinstein at the 1975 Euclid Conference: "problem solving, estimation, ability to use calculators and computers intelligently, data analysis, understanding of probabilistic concepts, and geometric intuition." The authors sought to build on what students already knew about math. Otherwise, added Carl Bereiter, "There is a danger that they will not see any connection themselves – will fail to see school mathematics as relevant to their understanding of the world." A *Real Math* problem might require students to make a rough estimate, or to realize that there was not enough information available to reach an answer at all!

What was the correct label for such an approach? At first, the authors thought of themselves as writing a back-to-basics program, in opposition to the overly conceptual "new math." Then in 1975 Macmillan came out with a back-to-basics program that Rubinstein describes as "just computation problems between hard covers. You couldn't call it a math program. It was hardly even an arithmetic program." This was nothing like the thinking program the authors had in mind – and as Steve Willoughby wrote, it was a dead end: "Using psychological theories of the 1920s to teach skills thought useful in the 1890s is hardly appropriate in the 1980s."

Whatever it might be called, the authors were pleased with the *Real Math* process and the result, and with Blouke's willingness to pay for it. The complete program was published in 1981, and revised and extended to eighth grade in 1985. "We paid little attention to traditional marketing wisdom," says Rubinstein. Marketing would have dictated that they produce a fashionable and saleable back-to-basics program. Blouke, who faithfully attended the quarterly math meetings, backed the authors up, recalls Rubinstein.

The authors' seemingly infinite capacity for taking pains won them professional prestige. In 1980, the National Council of Teachers of Mathematics issued an *Agenda for Action,* whose first three proposals – that "problem solving be the focus of school mathematics," that "basic skills in mathematics be defined to encompass more than computational facility," and that "mathematics programs take full advantage of the power of calculators and computers at all grade levels" – echoed the *Real Math* philosophy. Willoughby himself was elected president of NCTM in 1981. In October 1989, after NCTM had issued *Curriculum and Evaluation Standards* in much the same vein, André Carus noted that the group would "direct newspapers to *Real Math* schools as sites exemplifying the implementation" of those standards. Many of those who worked on math for Open Court went on to senior math editorial positions at other publishing houses.

But Open Court and the authors did not reap comparable rewards in the marketplace. On behalf of Random House, George Rosato declined to join Open Court in marketing the program, even though he agreed "this is the way math should be taught." He thought it could work only with advanced learners and top-notch teachers. A subsequent small "learner verification" study by Robert Dilworth of the California Institute of Technology and Leonard Warren of the San-Diego-based Center for the Improvement of Mathematics Education found otherwise. If anything, *Real Math* students from lower and middle socio-economic levels outscored upper-class children.

As in reading, for many educators it was a problem that Open Court math was an instructional system that did not lend itself to the eclectic approach often adopted by teachers. According to *Curriculum Review,* "*Real Math* asks the teacher to adopt a curricular philosophy." Similarly, the Thomas Nelson & Sons reviewer said, "*Real Math* is all or nothing – either the guide is . . . used faithfully alongside all of the ancillary goodies or the program is incomplete and far less effective." According to Willoughby, most of Open Court's own sales staff felt that the program asked too much, while he and Blouke insisted their program was better than anything else on the market. Both groups were right.

Even in the earliest math tryouts – with interested teachers and supportive schools – Open Court's Joe Rubinstein found teachers supplementing *Real Math* with other materials. In later years the company had to supply extra practice sheets to teachers who refused to believe that kids could learn any other way. In 1983, the Chicago Public Schools math supervisor told Blouke that she preferred to pick and choose from many programs. His response was classic Open Court: "If teachers do that . . . they invariably omit the hard and necessary elements, and we do not like to see this."

8. Working bottom-up and top-down (1975–1985)

"Policymakers determined to improve public schooling face a paradox in viewing the teacher as both the cause of school problems and the indispensable source of a solution. . . . Unless those teachers are enlisted in the effort to alter past practices, unless they understand new knowledge, unless their beliefs are transformed, and unless they develop new skills, little will improve in classrooms." – Larry Cuban, *How Teachers Taught*

TEACHERS

THERE SHE WAS – the veteran first-grade teacher, the last person Mary Burkhardt wanted to see at the post office on Christmas Eve 1974. Burkhardt had had a busy fall since being appointed director of reading for the Rochester, New York, school district. The district had adopted three new intensive-phonics reading programs – Open Court, Distar, and Lippincott – and trained teachers in their use. During those months Burkhardt and the first-grade teacher had crossed paths in local drugstores and supermarkets. Each time she gave Burkhardt an earful about what a mistake the district was making. Rather than raise Rochester students' abysmal reading scores, the teacher insisted, the new programs would lower them even more, because too many kids were unable (as she put it) to "learn phonetically."

Now they were face-to-face in the bustling post office. "Mrs. Burkhardt, I just have one thing to tell you." Burkhardt took a deep breath and braced herself for the worst. "I have taught reading in this district for 20 years, but my first graders have never been as far advanced as my students are this year. I just *thought* I was teaching reading before!"

This story suggests why Open Court never quite made up its

mind whether teachers were heroes or villains. They were key to Blouke's never-abandoned idea of selling Open Court by contagion; they were also the stick-in-the-muds who resisted it.

"We are perceived as intricate by teachers," mused general manager Howard Webber in 1982, "and they do not welcome intricacy, even if it is accompanied by success for them and their children." He quoted one teacher: "Many teachers say [Open Court] is too difficult for the kids. Actually, it's too difficult for the teachers."

"Teachers tend to select what is attractive," Blouke lamented in 1990. "They tend to look for the latest fads, they only consider textbooks if they have a recent copyright, they tend to look for materials that are easy to use rather than choose materials that consistently produce student learning gains. Unfortunately, therefore, the so-called 'market' has in general not been a market for instructional integrity nor for improving results."

The 1985 federal report *Becoming a Nation of Readers* offered a dispiriting explanation why Open Court's customers were not all they might have been. "College students who choose education as a major have lower average scores on a number of indices of ability than students who select other majors. Among students who begin an education program, those who complete the program have less ability than those who switch to other programs. Among college graduates who get teaching certificates, those who seek teaching jobs are less talented than those who do not. Most alarming of all, among people who take jobs as teachers, those who remain in teaching after five years are less able than those who leave to enter other fields."

These numbers no doubt reflect what a commission of the American Association of Colleges for Teacher Education found in 1976 and again in 1985 – that there are "marked" discrepancies between the condition of teaching and the condition of a true profession. "Central is the relative absence [in teaching] of a validated body of knowledge and skills subscribed to by the profession, passed by means of preparation programs to the inductees, and used as the basis for determining entrance to and continuance in the profession." Together, education's low pay and lack of professionalism probably encouraged well-educated middle-class

women to seek challenging employment elsewhere as the twentieth century rolled on and other arenas became open to them.

Again, in July 1982, the members of the Pittsburgh reading
committee said they would like to use Open Court themselves,
but declined to recommend it for system-wide adoption because
the teachers wouldn't do that much work. Blouke saw a similar
problem in mathematics. At one point he went so far as to suggest
that the company try mobilizing "our natural allies, the mathematics professors and the senior high school math teachers, and
encourage them to take an interest in, and if possible to get
involved in, local elementary school mathematics adoptions."

Even in the earliest grades, where Open Court was strongest,
teachers frequently gutted or misused the program. "Both the
first- and second-grade teachers felt that there were many components of the program that they 'simply didn't have time for,'"
Janice Baker and Naomi Zigmund of the University of Pittsburgh
wrote in *Exceptional Children,* examining one urban school in the
late 1980s. "Three of the four teachers had eliminated the composition cycle from the reading instruction routine. One teacher
'couldn't fit' the Response Card Drills into the phonics lesson
sequence. . . . The comprehension workbooks provided with the
series were judged to be too hard and to require too much
teacher direction." Astonishingly, "in all K-2 classrooms, lessons
were taught to the whole class; there was no grouping for instruction" – i.e., no Workshop.

It was not news to Open Court that some teachers did this –
but the company needed the sales! At one point André concluded, "It is better for a district to use *our* program badly (with *our*
collateral materials, producing income for us), if that gives even
one teacher the opportunity for genuine cultural upgrading, than
for that *opportunity* not to exist."

Teachers' anticipated responses limited the design of Open
Court programs as well as their sale. When the reading program
was under revision in the middle 1980s, André reiterated the
need for the company to provide detailed lesson plans. "What our
informal evidence tells us . . . is that teachers must have a routine,
and must be given precise, concrete instructions where they are

to do anything that deviates from 'standard practice' (a combination of teacher lore and what they learned in teachers' college). They can follow a recipe. They are not equipped to extrapolate from 'examples' or 'models' of what they might do or say." Certainly the midwesterners who met with Mary Jane Ketch at exhibits and in-services during October 1985 were not: "Just about any teacher using Open Court at second and third grade asked when we would have workshop activity books for them. I hope we reconsider publishing these. It would also solve many problems regarding workshop and produce some sales."

Likewise, when the company contemplated adding a step to its composition cycle, André was dubious. Open Court teachers, he said, were "already overtaxed intellectually by sentence-lifting the way it is. We are being asked for brief teacher-handbooks on punctuation, spelling, grammar, and the like. How are we going to expect teachers to grapple with distinguishing good from bad writing?"

TOP-DOWN

Trying to change the education culture from the top down had not been Blouke's original plan. Nevertheless the company sometimes felt it had no choice. In 1995 Jerry Lebo advised Open Court salespeople to seek out schools and districts that had (among other things) strong leadership focused on improving teaching; math or reading specialists; adoption committees to choose textbooks rather than all-teacher votes; and adoption committees with parents as members. In other words, salespeople were to target places where teachers as a group had less influence.

What few accountability mechanisms exist in American public education have usually operated at the building, district, or state level, rather than the individual classroom. Many school districts choose textbooks (and thus in effect curricula) system-wide. Rochester in 1974 was such a district, one in which the school board was under political pressure to improve low reading scores. The board insisted on a top-down change that Mary Burkhardt's veteran teacher, for one, would never have endorsed on her own.

In districts like Rochester, Open Court did not depend on a grass-roots following, but on sympathetic and thorough instructional supervisors. Walter VanMeeteren of Plymouth Christian School in Michigan outlined the situation in a letter to Blouke August 31, 1971: "I feel that a teacher has to discipline herself to the realistic fact that she is going to have to *follow* the [Open Court] program for success. She is going to have to teach it for a whole year before she can appreciate and understand [it]. . . . She has to be an individual who is ambitious, because that first year is hard work. I've had teachers dislike it with a passion the first 6 weeks because it was too demanding, however, those that followed the program as intended, soon changed their attitude – those that have not followed the teacher's guide never did like the program and as a result found little success and neither did the students."

By approximately 1980, Open Court was being used in all thirty-five Rochester elementary schools. In each building a reading teacher trained and supervised teachers. (A similar system worked well in Canton, Ohio, in the early 1970s, where the district paid two full-time "helping teachers" to work with Open Court teachers in grades 1 through 5.) But after Burkhardt left the school system in 1981, budget cuts eliminated the extra reading teachers. Principals moved on and their successors didn't notice when teachers began to modify parts of the program and omit others. Years earlier, the school board had provoked improvement – but because there was no ongoing accountability mechanism, once conditions improved, no one had an incentive to maintain the good practices that created the improvement in the first place.

"During school visitations I discovered that the program was being modified greatly in many buildings," Gretchen Toole reported to Blouke in late 1986. "Classroom materials either did not exist or were not being used . . . and, in general, teachers were just biding time waiting to hear what 'new' program would be adopted." Union rules made it impossible to require training of teachers or administrators. By the mid-1980s Open Court was in serious trouble in Rochester. A local newspaper was able to find plenty of discontented teachers who portrayed Open Court as "for a middle class or upper-middle class student body."

In 1976–77, when Blouke tried working down from the top in one state education system, he didn't even get far enough to experience the need for constant follow-up. Michigan Superintendent of Public Instruction John Porter had championed high standards and accountability, and had spoken to Open Court's Educational Advisory Board in 1974. Blouke called him "one of the best Superintendents of Public Instruction in the USA." But when Blouke offered to furnish Open Court materials free to selected Michigan schools – and guarantee their performance – Porter's office provided more bureaucratic hurdles than support. What was an "open-court" classroom? Michigan educrats wondered. How could their office compel local schools to use a particular commercial program?

Eventually a deal was approved at the state level. Porter communicated it tepidly to school superintendents in Lansing and Grand Rapids, introducing them to Blouke and Open Court: "He and his staff believe Open Court's approach to reading and staff training can make a significant difference in the basic skills performance of children in high needs schools. They are so convinced of the power of their program, the company is willing to provide materials and training on a pilot basis to three high need buildings . . . free of charge for one year." Porter had no authority to compel local superintendents to try something new, and showed little interest in even encouraging them to do so. He left the initiative up to them, and nothing came of it.

Even at the local level a top-down approach could fail. Math author Stephen Willoughby described the course of events in one large city: "The professional educators went through a careful evaluation of all available textbook series and chose three (all of which I believe were good). The city board of education chose to add a fourth (very mediocre) series because the sales representative from that company was a leader in the church that several of the members attended. That fourth program required no change on the part of teachers and became the best seller in the city."

Getting Open Court into the schools, and keeping it properly taught once there, thus could often seem like rolling a stone uphill. One moment of inattention – a principal transferred here, a company financial crisis leading to a cutback on consultants there – and all efforts might come to naught.

Such problems were not peculiar to Open Court, as Blouke was wont to emphasize to Open Court people by quoting Machiavelli: "There is nothing more difficult to take in hand, more perilous to conduct, or more uncertain in its success, than to take the lead in the introduction of a new order of things." In her 1990 essay, "They Shake but Nothing Moves: A Social Scientist Looks at Educational Reform," Sheila Tobias amplified his point. "Innovations tend to disappear when . . . the committed progenitor moves on to other things."

Similarly, in his book *Schoolhouse Politics: Lessons from the Sputnik Era,* Peter Dow cites Lynne Falkenstein's research, which centered on the innovative and controversial curriculum called "Man: A Course of Study" (MACOS). Open Court was rarely controversial in the way that MACOS was. But Falkenstein's general findings seem to apply to Open Court's situation as well. She found that innovations "were bound to falter regardless of their quality," unless administrators provided teachers with support and training beyond the initial implementation phase. The greatest barrier to innovation was not controversial subject matter. It was a lack of accountability, aka "lack of continuity of support from the internal structure of the school system itself."

BOTTOM-UP

In the mid-1980s, Open Court tried out a different version of its old demonstration centers in the guise of foundation-funded "piloting projects" linked to what Blouke called the "Excellence Movement." By funding such trials, the company argued, "Foundations can break down barriers against research-based educational innovation, and improve educational practice, literacy, test-scores, and morale, even in the inner cities. . . . In our experience, pilots lead to more widespread acceptance of Open Court programs in about 50% of all cases."

Blouke's strategy in the 1980s remained much as it had been twenty years earlier: reach a "vanguard" of good teachers and the rest would follow. "Even the most traditional and conservative school systems have innovators among the teacher staff who are willing to try the new methods. And once they have produced good results, the majority is much more willing to go along with a major change." In this way, "the textbook adoption process, for years perhaps the major obstacle to educational change (and possibly the main reason for the failure of the 1960's curriculum projects), would be overcome by the creation of a constituency for change *among the teachers themselves.*"

That's what happened in Wheeling, West Virginia, in 1982, according to a report in the Weirton, West Virginia, *Times* (1/17/83). "Wheeling's original demonstration project was to include only 29 first-graders at North Park [School]. Teachers from schools all over the county were invited to observe the use of the program in case they should later want to use it in their own classes. The reaction of North Park second- and third-grade teachers was immediate and dramatic. They went to Principal Fassig and Rosemary Coury, reading supervisor, and asked that the program be made available to their students right away. The results being produced in the first grade were so impressive that they did not want to wait until the next school year to see similar results in their grades."

Larger systems proved more resistant to Blouke's idea of an ever-expanding vanguard. The Chicago school board approved a pilot of Open Court's language arts program *Headway* in May 1986, for about twenty volunteer schools involving a total of about 10,000 students. This was already inconsistent with Blouke's idea of individual classrooms being the unit of piloting, but there was worse to come. Chicago bureaucracy precluded timely teacher training. As late as August 12, associate superintendent Margaret Harrigan was insisting that no preparations could go forward before the contract mentioned by the board had been executed, according to André Carus's account. And then "she refused to specify what terms this contract should contain," referring him to the legal department.

Meanwhile foundations proved resistant to Blouke's pitch that since neither Open Court nor school districts could afford to fund large-scale pilots themselves, the foundations should seize "an opportunity to . . . leave a lasting effect on the literacy, numeracy, and thinking skills of American youth." With less money

raised than expected, Open Court had to reduce the Chicago
pilot's size. And then September's teacher training alerted Jerry
Lebo to the fact that Chicago teachers in no way resembled
Blouke's vision of a vanguard. They would need additional training of the most basic kind. "The idea of teaching the whole group
and then working with subgroups on the same story" – integral to
Open Court – "was completely foreign to many of these teachers.
We'll need to put in much more time and effort to get that concept across."

Lebo's warnings soon became strident. "We have stepped into
the quicksand," he reported in November after spending three
days at the Chicago pilot schools, "and will disappear in it unless
we take immediate and forceful action to make something out of
these pilots." Only one principal cared about the pilot's success,
and only three teachers understood Open Court's philosophy
and procedures. "The teachers control by force. It never occurs to
them to praise, to ensure success, or to motivate in any way. They
have all the spirit and excitement of baked halibut. Even when
you show them that the kids react well to spirited teaching, they
go right back into the same mode." Worse yet, Chicago's outcome
testing program did not mesh well with Open Court's *Headway*.

One kindergarten teacher had already abandoned the pilot.
"She says, in the same breath, that her kids have already surpassed
what is in the program, and that they can't do the activities."
Another had posted twenty-six A-Z wall sound cards "on and
around the windows in no particular order" (having apparently
done away with the cards representing the other eighteen
sounds!). Lebo recommended that the company hire a consultant to visit each building every day for the remainder of the
school year, and that some way be found to arrange for weaker
teachers to observe good teaching at their grade level. Since that
kind of visiting and contagion had been the rationale for piloting
in the first place, it was obvious that something had gone badly
wrong in its implementation.

BOTH WAYS

Perhaps the ideal situation combined support from above and

below. In Berkeley, California, in the early 1980s, instructional services director Beverly Maimoni managed a successful district-wide mathematics adoption procedure. "What I found," she wrote later, "was that you had to make all of the conditions right if you wanted to make a transition between a traditional program and one that had some other facets to it." She gave the adoption committee (teachers and parents) both time and training – in the person of an actual mathematician from San Francisco State, who was able to explain that, for instance, teaching problem- solving is not the same thing as giving students a worksheet full of word problems. Ultimately the committee voted 23-4 for *Real Math,* provided that it be piloted and that principals receive in-service training in it as well.

When the program went into effect district-wide, Maimoni had two consultants work with the teachers while she stayed in the background. "Teachers were finding reasons not to use these new materials. 'I never teach addition and subtraction at the same time;' or 'I always teach to mastery, I'm not going to move on until the students have mastered this concept.' 'Oh – it's too noisy to use the cube games on the mats. I can't hear when all of that is going on.' 'I don't have time to count out all of the money before we play a game.'" In response, Maimoni collected suggestions from more successful teachers and wrote them up in a handbook of tips, which "seemed to provide a real lift to the teachers." So did grade-level meetings among teachers.

"My persuasion," Maimoni concluded, "admittedly subjective from the classes I have visited, is that minority youngsters do far better in the Open Court [math program] than they do in the traditional paper-and-pencil programs. This is because *Real Math* is a language program and a thinking program." But her liking for the program did not blind her to the need for "buy-in," as summarized from the business-change literature by Sheila Tobias: "The innovator must work as hard on ensuring that a set of *supportive peers* exists as on designing the innovation itself." Without a cultural change, there could be no lasting educational change.

9. Research, Resistance, Renewal (1978–1985)

"Teachers have not been guided in applying reliable research to the design of classroom instruction; the reliable research has been lost in a welter of inferior stuff; promising pedagogical approaches are relatively little used; in most schools, classroom success can only with difficulty be distinguished from classroom failure; and little movement has been made in improving students' reading skills." – Blouke Carus, August 12, 1980

THE NEW EDUCATIONAL RESEARCH

IN THE BEGINNING, Open Court's textbooks were not based on educational research, other than the Gurren-Hughes report and the Hegeler Project of the middle 1960s, described in Chapters 3 and 4. What other research existed was mediocre or didn't agree with Blouke's views. In 1974, at Blouke's request, four top managers assembled a list of the Open Court's ten greatest strengths. Being based on research was not one of them.

Open Court's reformist stance did give it more respect for expertise than the average textbook publisher had, and a less-than-average willingness to make concessions to easy marketability. As a result, the company gained a reputation for being willing to let top professionals write textbooks as they judged best. During the late 1960s and early 1970s, writes Stephen Willoughby, "I explained to representatives of many major textbook publishers what I wanted to do. Seven of the publishers offered me a senior authorship and an opportunity to become very rich if I would not do what I wanted to do. They all wanted a 'new math' or a 'back-to-basics' program that would be published two to three years after the contracts were signed [and hence could not be adequately tested in schools] and that would look familiar and easy for teachers. I would be allowed to influence but not actually control the final product. Usually I wasn't even expected to do much of the writing." When Willoughby met Blouke in 1972, he was astonished to find a publisher who not only would allow him to write the textbook of which he would be named as the author, but who also would expect him to do so according to his own lights.

Open Court did embrace some research as time when by as when it embraced Jean Chall's path-breaking book and worked closely with Carl Bereiter. But not until the end of the 1970s did research come to play a major, explicit part in Open Court's self-image. General Manager Howard Webber's 1978 plan included in Open Court's mission the task of "developing educational materials . . . that are based on research findings." Blouke praised a 1981 conference in terms that made it clear that he had been proceeding largely on his own judgment: "I consider the Tarrytown seminar a very important event in the history of American education. *At last* a group of well-informed, research-based, highly respected scholars were able to make formal presentations from many important points of view to the major textbook publishers. Fortunately for our side, the messages more or less confirmed our own intuitions."

"More or less" is right. The research on beginning reading, summarized by Joanna Williams of Teachers College, Columbia University, in 1981, leaned Open Court's way but not unequivocally so. "Sometimes, decoding-emphasis approaches lead to significantly greater achievement on reading tests. The effects, when they occur, show up only in the early grades and are seen only when word recognition is assessed. The effects are more likely to appear when children of low socioeconomic level are studied. Also, the effects, when they occur, are never very large. [Blouke attributes this to inadequate school management.] The empirical evidence, however, never leans in the other direction; there are no studies in which reading programs that do not emphasize decoding are superior."

In the 1970s, a new generation of researchers coming from allied fields like linguistics, cognitive psychology, and computer science – Bereiter among them – took a fresh look at educational practices. Few asked how best to teach reading right at the start. That question seemed well settled academically, whatever might be going on in classrooms. Besides, the National Institute of Education avoided the hot-button issue of phonics. As a result, researchers focused on reading comprehension. In what quickly became a cliché, they moved from "learning to read" to "reading to learn." Their work was aided when the National Institute of Education began contracting with university centers such as the Center for the Study of Reading at the University of Illinois in the middle 1970s. The exhortation and simple description that had dominated educational research gradually gave way to description informed by theory, and theory informed by controlled studies that could pass muster in the social sciences.

One breakthrough was schema theory – in brief, the idea that people understand what they read by fitting it into patterns that they already know. Consider the sentence, "The big number 37 smashed the ball over the fence." As schema theory pioneer and director of the Center for the Study of Reading Richard Anderson points out, you are not likely to understand this sentence unless you can place it within the schema of baseball. This may sound like common sense, but it contradicts the equally common-sensical theory described by Anderson, according to which "comprehension consists of aggregating the meaning of words to form the meanings of clauses, aggregating the meaning of clauses to form the meanings of sentences, aggregating the meanings of sentences to form the meanings of paragraphs, and so on." In contrast, he argues, "The meanings of the words cannot be 'added up' to give the meaning of the whole. The click of comprehension occurs only when the reader evolves a schema that explains the whole message."

Schema theory implies that students will understand any given passage better if they know beforehand what pattern to fit it into. Thus American high-schoolers were found to do much better at reading and recalling newspaper reports of cricket matches if they first were taught something about the game. This led to the now-standard practice known as "activating prior knowledge" before reading. One relatively primitive way of doing this in the classroom was to reverse the order of two familiar tasks and have students read over the comprehension questions before reading the story. (As we will see, Open Court was trying to do away with comprehension questions altogether, with only partial success.) But the University of Arizona's Virginia Richardson, writing in *Educational Researcher* (October 1990), found in her research that teachers' rationale for this practice had nothing to do with schema theory or the growth of understanding. Instead, its purpose was "consistently expressed as making sure the students got the right answers and did better on the tests." In this instance teachers followed the research without knowing about it, much as their students performed activities without understanding what they were supposed to learn from them.

TEACH HIGH-LEVEL SKILLS, OR EXERCISE THEM?

Educators had long been under the impression that teachers were imparting high-order skills. A popular basal series claimed to teach "identifying picture details, story details, supporting details, main ideas, and referents; sequencing; drawing conclusions; predicting outcomes; inferring causes and effects; and making comparisons" up through sixth grade.

Carl Bereiter and Marlene Scardamalia saw that this emperor had no clothes on. "Every normal child entering school can already do all of these things. A child could hardly carry on a conversation if this were not the case. Consequently, none of them needs to be taught – which is fortunate, since the program offers no clue as to how any of them might be taught to a child who happened to lack one of them. Although the basal programs, and teachers themselves, often speak of 'teaching' these competencies, what they in fact refer to almost exclusively is *exercising* them."

The work of Dolores Durkin of the University of Illinois' Center for the Study of Reading confirmed this stunning indictment. Durkin had observed 11,587 minutes of reading classes, and found that just 45 minutes – less than one percent of total class time – was spent on teaching comprehension. Ten times more minutes were spent assessing comprehension than teaching it! "Instead of being instructors, the 39 observed teachers were mentioners, assignment givers, assignment checkers, and interrogators."

Even when teachers were supposedly dealing with high-level cognitive functions, the activities crowded out the goal. "What is the reason for relying on practice to teach instead of on direct, explicit instruction, which is then followed by practice?" asked Durkin, poking the education culture with a sharp stick. "More generally, why are means so often treated as ends in themselves?"

Jean Osborn of the Center for the Study of Reading examined major publishers' workbooks and found that they too concentrated on activity to the exclusion of understanding. One egregious Houghton Mifflin syllabication exercise gave students a number of words, each printed inside a rectangular, square, or triangular outline, and asked students to color the outlines according to the number of syllables, then cut them out and assemble each color group so as to form squares! Linguist Alice Davison found that use of popular readability formulas often led textbook authors to shorten sentences and omit connectives in ways that made the text harder rather than easier to understand. Readability formulas were "the real devil," recalls Blouke. "We just couldn't break their hold. It was the whole-language movement [see chapter 11] that did that."

In this context, the discovery that comprehension strategies could be taught was a major breakthrough. In a paper published in the 1984 volume *Learning to Read in American Schools: Basal Readers and Content Texts,* Bonnie Armbruster and Ann Brown advocated "cognitive training with awareness," which included teaching students strategies like self-questioning and summarizing. Most current reading instruction, they said, consisted of "blind training," in which students "are induced to follow a rule or use a strategy without a concurrent understanding of the significance of that activity." Thus students could do well in school without ever learning how to learn.

Much of the new reading research was summarized for public consumption in the 1985 book, *Becoming a Nation of Readers,* the report of the national Commission on Reading, which Richard Anderson chaired. On key points the commission report affirmed practices that Open Court had pioneered before they had research behind them: intensive phonics (including plenty of practice blending sounds and reading decodable text), direct teaching, not relying on readability formulas, and not grouping children by ability.

Becoming a Nation of Readers did not confirm all of Blouke's theories. His original belief that improved reading instruction could raise the level of all schooling by a couple of years did not fare well under investigation. "By sixth grade, the group that years earlier had received intensive phonics instruction still did better than the comparison group on a word identification test but the [earlier] advantage in comprehension had vanished." Overall the company liked *Becoming a Nation of Readers* well enough to use its issuance as the news peg for a promotional press release. André wrote, "Only a few years ago, researchers lacked a very precise idea of what these crucial strategies are that separate good from poor readers and writers. Now many have been pinpointed and isolated, and we even have quite a good idea of how they can be taught."

"SUBSTANTIALLY MISREPRESENTED"

The researchers assumed a consensus on beginning reading that did not exist. Open Court's major 1979 reading revision, called *Headway,* drew a misleading review from Michael Strange (University of Texas, Austin) and Margaret Rice (Leander Independent School District, Texas) in the March 1980 *Reading Teacher.* Strange and Rice made the program seem narrower than it was, largely omitting its emphasis on writing and the way in which oral and spelling skills were integrated into the program. They focused on the Foundation portion (the first semester of first grade) on the grounds that "it is at that level that the program is most different from others currently available."

Headway, they concluded, "is most definitely a synthetic phonics approach and consequently is open for criticism from those who feel that reading is best taught from a meaning emphasis.

They will find much of what is done during each lesson distasteful and will be unable to give it the enthusiasm and careful preparation that this program requires." (One might argue that many
professionals find some part of their practice distasteful, without
drawing the conclusion that they can get along without it!) With
a final tip of the hat to pick-and-choose, Strange and Rice concluded that "in the hands of a good teacher using the many fine
parts of the program, it should be successful."

On March 21, Open Court publisher Howard Webber and
curriculum director Dale Howard fired off a three-and-one-half-
page single-spaced reply. In a phone call to editor Janet Binkley
and in an accompanying letter, Webber asked her to publish the
reply "very promptly," because "we are not dwelling on a mere difference of opinion. A central program of ours has been substantially misrepresented, and that will have educational and economic consequences over the summer that could touch us very
deeply," he wrote. "I suppose I end by believing that you have a
professional responsibility to give us an adequate platform to state
our case." He said he would consider purchasing an ad if necessary, but he shouldn't have to: "We ought to be given the opportunity to redress the errors of omission and assertion it makes."

Binkley's own concept of professional responsibility may be
inferred from the fact that she cut three-quarters of their reply
and didn't publish the remainder until October, well after the
end of that year's selling season.

How badly were Strange, Rice, and Binkley missing the boat?
Pretty badly, to judge from Barbara Eckhoff's 1985 Ed.D. thesis in
Harvard's Graduate School of Education. Eckhoff found that
what children read affected how they wrote. "Perhaps the most
important finding is that the *Open Court* children compared to the
Ginn children tended to use more the linguistically complex sentence structures that they have found in their texts, such as subordinate clauses, infinitive phrases, and participial phrases.
Children who use these structures in their writing are better able
to express complex ideas and relationships than children who are
limited to simpler structures."

RESISTING RESEARCH AT THE TOP

In his capacity as head of the nonprofit Hegeler Foundation, Blouke agreed to join with other funders to defray the cost of another conference to spread the word about the new research. "Foundations for a Literate America" was held in March 1982 at Wingspread, sponsored by the University of Illinois's Center for the Study of Reading. Presenters included Durkin, Bereiter, Ann Brown, Jean Osborn, Roger Farr, Douglas Carnine, and other researchers. Its proceedings were published in a twenty-four-chapter volume, *Reading Education: Foundations for a Literate America,* in 1985. It seemed an unlikely target for vituperative attack.

Comprehension was again a focus at Wingspread. James Cunningham of the University of North Carolina drew practical maxims from the relevant research: "To help readers comprehend better, teachers should do the following: 1. Have students read easy materials and perform comprehension tasks that can be completed with high success. 2. Teach concepts for topics and words. 3. Use tested interventions [such as previewing and self-questioning] to guide students' reading during comprehension lessons." He remarked quizzically, "As a veteran provider of in-service comprehension instruction training, I have yet to find a group of elementary teachers in which many know about the directed reading-thinking activity, the guided reading procedure, or the ReQuest procedure."

Shortly after the apparent success of the Wingspread conference, International Reading Association executive director Ralph Staiger circulated a two-page memorandum to IRA board members and to Richard Anderson, the head of the Center for the Study of Reading. Staiger questioned the conference's intellectual integrity and hinted that it had been corrupt. He said it had been one-sided, had failed to acknowledge the limitations of the research ("in reality, there is much that is still not known"), and had overemphasized "one kind of direct instruction." Open Court authors, consultants, and staff were, he wrote, "very evident on the program and in the audience. . . . For a number of people, the 'he who pays the piper calls the tune' attitude damaged the credibility of the meeting."

The memo infuriated Anderson, who in a lengthy reply denied that any funders had input into what was said at Wingspread, and accused Staiger of malicious inconsistency. "No reasonable person would find it odd that staff of a publishing company attended a conference sponsored in part by an affiliated charitable foundation. What is truly odd is that the executive officer of an organization that professes to represent the entire reading community in a fair and even-handed manner [i.e., the IRA] believes that participation in a conference by the employees of one publishing company is sinister whereas participation by those of another company [Ginn, which Staiger had not mentioned] is benign." Anderson pointed out that conference presenters held a variety of views and asked why Staiger seemed to have "set out to fan the flames of ideological passion within the field."

Anderson drew a blunt conclusion. "IRA is an ideological Trojan horse. Its officers pretend that it is an open professional and scholarly organization when in fact it is the property of a ruling clique that defends a certain orthodoxy about reading. Within that orthodoxy to invite Douglas Carnine to a meeting is ipso facto to demonstrate 'bias'; a report on synthetic phonics is 'detached and impartial' only if it comes to the conclusion that the practice is ineffective or harmful to children. I reject your orthodoxy."

Staiger would not be drawn into battle. He responded quietly, professing surprise at Anderson's anger and claiming that he merely "saw and heard some danger signals, and commented on them to you."

Staiger did not win the argument; James Squire of Ginn wrote that he didn't perceive any undue influence. But in order to shore up the reading status quo and defend the education culture, Staiger didn't have to win. All he needed to do was to minimize the value of the research results presented and make sure that the opinion leaders on the IRA board knew to do the same. He didn't need to prolong the controversy or make a permanent enemy of Anderson. Having poisoned the well, he could step back.

The IRA itself remained unchanged. As E. Jennifer Monaghan of Brooklyn College of the City University of New York told a session of the group's meeting on reading research in 1997, the IRA had "never, during the more than forty years of its existence, published a single work that instructs its members either on the phonology and orthography of their own language or of ways in which this knowledge might be presented to children."

RESISTING RESEARCH AT THE GRASS ROOTS

Open Court editor Dale Howard gazed into the abyss between research and reality at a September 1982 conference in Tarrytown. Andee Rubin of Bolt Beranek & Newman reviewed studies showing how readability formulas devastate the quality of text. Nancy Sargeant of Houghton Mifflin responded, saying, "That's all very good, but now for the real world" – meaning the world of publishing and selling, not research. To Howard's consternation, she got the biggest applause of the conference.

Sargeant's point surely was that teachers and administrators would rarely consider, let alone purchase, textbooks that did not use readability formulas. Open Court took serious economic risks when it refused to abide by them.

The company ventured even further ahead of its customers (not to mention its critics) in *Headway*. There it introduced new kinds of comprehension activities that did not rely on students' mechanically answering questions supplied after each selection.

There had been no customer demand for this improvement, but the company was sure it was educationally necessary. "Comprehension questions do the child's wondering for him, so to speak," Carl Bereiter wrote. "He allows his attention to be guided passively by them. Thus they encourage the child to be a more passive reader and, paradoxically train him not to use the very skills they are trying to teach."

Open Court was guided by an ideal – to make students lifelong independent learners – that most educators agreed with verbally. But even its own customers failed to make the connection between those lofty ideals and what they found in its textbooks. "There was a perception that we had no comprehension," recalls Karen

Hansill, a veteran of sales and management. "We did not have multiple worksheets for each selection. We'd have one worksheet, the other companies would have three or four. We had more teaching and discussion – but they'd rather assign it than teach it."

Hansill and colleagues spent the rest of the company's life responding to these objections. So did Blouke. "Teachers have become so used to workbooks," he wrote in 1984, "that they cannot understand that writing exercises and the comprehension exercises in *Headway,* and the mental arithmetic, thinking stories, and math games in *Real Math,* provide much more drill and practice with a much more efficient use of classroom time than is possible with workbooks."

Again in 1985, André wondered, "Are there any teachers (or administrators) anywhere that are prepared to accept anything other than questioning as constituting 'comprehension'? . . . We hear rumors from the educational research community that the old ideas about comprehension are all but dead, and that 'all programs' are now abandoning questioning; our experience in the field suggests this can't be true." It wasn't. Reflecting on his experience years later, André said, "There was probably never a sales meeting or Field Advisory Board meeting from 1979 to 1996 at which the sales force (including consultants) didn't demand comprehension questions, and at which we didn't have to explain all over again why they were a bad idea."

GETTING INTO HIGH CULTURE

Researchers' move from "learning to read" toward "reading to learn" was good news for Open Court. At last, they were focusing their attention on Blouke's original motive for publishing textbooks at all: "to reach beyond the basics [not defined] to a high level of reading, writing, speaking, figuring, and thinking. At the same time, we want to nurture in children a joy for learning. In our basic readers we believe it is important that students develop an appreciation for the best of classical and modern writing for children. In elementary mathematics our objectives extend beyond the mastery of skills to solve *real* problems and to develop their mathematical intelligence."

Getting Open Court converts to move "beyond the mastery of skills" and appreciate the value of cultural upgrading proved exceptionally difficult. In 1970, fewer than half of the schools using Open Court in first grade continued it through fourth grade. Throughout the 1980s, more than half the company's sales were in kindergarten and first grade.

Those who were happy to use Open Court in the early grades often found fault with later years' books, when they used them at all. In March 1974 in Richmond, California, teachers at Valley View objected to the later grades' books' "difficult vocabulary," "archaic words," and "most uninviting" appearance. "Early stories (Greek mythology) 'kill interest' before we get to better, more interesting stories. Comprehension much beyond average 4, 5, 6 graders." And in his 1971 letter, as warm a sympathizer as Walter VanMeeteren of Plymouth Christian School in Michigan had made similar complaints. Open Court's program, he wrote, was "too demanding in some areas. . . . We have 95% positive reactions to the program from K through 3. However, sit down sometime and read the 4th grade Reader from an average 4th grade *boy's* frame of reference."

VanMeeteren may have thought his point was marginal to Open Court. But that reader, *What Joy Awaits You,* embodied the company's core ambition. The Caruses had put it together in 1966 after visiting the Midwest Interlibrary Center's thousand feet of shelves containing readers from 1850 on. "We went through a dungeon of textbooks, all with a pile of dust on them," Blouke recalls. "We selected the best 10–20 feet of them and had them sent to our local library. It was terribly exciting looking through these old Beacon, Ginn, McGuffey, etc. readers, because they gave us a real feel for what students have read in the past and could read and understand at each grade level." Ultimately *What Joy Awaits You* included selections from Wordsworth, Blake, Tolstoy, Lewis Carroll, C.S. Lewis, Langston Hughes, Indian stories and legends, and many more. It made few concessions to its ten-year-old readers. One excerpt came straight from Captain John Smith's account of seventeenth-century Virginia. Its fifth- and sixth-grade counterparts were similar.

In 1973 an Open Court representative protested that "well over half the children in the room are not able to read with success in the series. The teacher is not prepared to handle this kind of material." Open Court editor Tom Anderson – himself no advocate of low culture – concluded in a 1975 memo that they had to go. "The intermediate program, even though the Readers contain many fine things, is a complete commercial failure. An entirely new set of Readers is needed in which due regard is paid to grade level." The new set came out in 1979 (the old ones remained available as an enrichment program called RISE) – ironically, just as other companies were beefing up their selections for the middle grades. The new versions, known as *Headway* readers H, I, and J, did not sell much better. Contrary to the usual pattern, they sold best in their first year, then started dropping. Open Court sales remained concentrated in first grade.

Clearly, making converts to phonics was one thing, and making converts to great literature was something else. As Blouke wrote to one correspondent in 1982, "We don't have many supporters who *really* understand one of our principal raisons d'être, so we especially appreciate those who do."

The anti-intellectual nature of the education culture was certainly part of the problem. But another big part was Open Court's. When Blouke and Marianne perused nineteenth-century readers and vowed to emulate them, they thought they were simply bringing back a high standard that had once existed for all children. But in fact those old texts had never led a majority of Americans to high culture. In those days most kids either didn't attend school at all or dropped out early to work. As late as 1910, more than half of the children who entered first grade had left school by sixth grade.

What Joy Awaits You never caught on because even the high-literacy tradition from Plato to McGuffey did not *teach* higher-order cognitive skills, it *assumed* them. "Students have been expected to read the works of the greatest writers and thinkers, and their own writing has been expected to reflect in some measure the qualities found in those works," wrote Carl Bereiter and Marlene Scardamalia in *Curriculum Inquiry* in 1987. "But the cognitive resources necessary for doing this have not been identified; much less have means been sought for developing them in students who did not already have them. Thus it is no wonder that coming from a literate background has been an important preliminary to acquiring high literacy." No wonder, too, that the Caruses' attempt to duplicate nineteenth-century readers for a larger population from less literate families had floundered, and that when Blouke was considering the grade 4–6 revision in 1976 he could only think in terms of "compromising" between Open Court's desire to transmit high culture and many students' manifest unreadiness for it.

To succeed in this unprecedented and daunting enterprise, Open Court could no longer go on intuition. The company would depend more on cutting-edge cognitive science than ever before.

TRANSCENDING PROGRESSIVISM AND TRADITIONALISM

Just as the new educational research vindicated many of Open Court's classroom practices, it also confirmed the company's underlying strategy – using both progressive and traditional practices as appropriate. In a 1983 paper entitled "Schooling and the Growth of Intentional Cognition: Helping Children Take Charge of Their Own Minds," Bereiter and Scardamalia drew on the metacognition research of Ann Brown and others to offer a deeper rationale for Blouke's pragmatism.

Intentional cognition as they define it is a person's ability to act rather than just react in the world of ideas. A person without intentional cognition may be able to think logically about a problem he or she finds interesting (or is assigned to deal with); a person with intentional cognition can *decide* that a given problem deserves that kind of attention. Again, a person without intentional cognition tries to find meaning in some part of the world; a person with intentional cognition tries to create meaning within the constraints the world provides. Intentional cognition is taking charge of cognition.

"In the absence of a clear understanding of what intentional

cognition is and how it develops," Bereiter and Scardamalia
wrote, "opposing viewpoints of a more-or-less philosophical
nature have grown up." In education, traditionalists emphasize
building knowledge and skills for future use, while progressives
emphasize the immediate exercise of autonomy. "Both of these
are reasonable approaches so long as one is obliged to treat the
child's developing mind as a black box. We know what we want to
come out of the box – independent thought, self-directed learning, willingness to tackle problems, and so on. We want to feed
things into the box that will yield these desired outputs.

"Knowing nothing about the mechanism that converts inputs
to outputs, we have two reasonable choices. One [traditionalism]
is to feed in constituents of the desired product. In this case, this
means feeding in general knowledge, logic skills, moral principles, etc. – all the elements that may be discerned in the mental
activity of mature adults. The other choice [progressivism] is to
nurture whatever appears to be an embryonic form of the desired
outcome. In this case it means nurturing the child's curiosity,
interests, self-assertiveness, and the like."

Now that the new research had gathered information on how
the "black box" worked, Bereiter and Scardamalia wrote, "We see
all the current approaches to education as defective and, more-
over, defective in essentially the same way." Progressive and traditional approaches alike seek to make learning arise "as a conse-
quence of natural behavior in the social environment of the
school." But this makes intentional cognition unnecessary!
"Whether child-centered or traditional in curriculum, whether
emphasizing work for extrinsic rewards or emphasizing activity
motivated by children's own interests, all the approaches aim to
create some kind of behavioral context where meaning, purpose,
and direction will inhere in the context. They all tend to minimize the need of children to construct mental lives of their own."

Neither free-wheeling discussion nor answering a list of "comprehension" questions helps students learn how to wrestle with a
text for meaning on their own. Having students memorize a list of
strategies wouldn't help either. In their 1987 paper, Bereiter and
Scardamalia added that the best alternative model for a school

they could think of was "the model of the learned professions. . . . [where] adaptation to the expectations of one's peers requires continual growth in knowledge and competence. . . . What the professional milieu supports is not a particular level of knowledge but rather a process of continually going beyond where one is." In the early stages of developing *Open Court Reading and Writing*, André produced a summary diagram of how Open Court hoped to move students from passive, teacher-dependent learning to active intentional learning. Thus, in the passive model, "Curiosity is aroused by novelty." In the active model, "Curiosity is aroused by discovered gaps in understanding of the ordinary."

The ideal school environment, then, would function like a learned profession, supporting continual growth in literacy. Idealistic, yes. Impossible, no. "A vital part of this idea has already been put into practice through one of the most successful efforts to upgrade literacy, the Bay Area Writing Project," wrote Bereiter and Scardamalia. "The part captured by that project is getting the teacher to function as a learner with respect to writing. Note that this is quite fundamentally different from the more common-place notion that the teacher of writing must be a good writer. Many teachers might be unable to meet that requirement. But the requirement that the teacher be able to function as a good learner of writing seems, to judge from the experience of the Bay Area project and its offshoots, to be within the capabilities of the majority."

In the 1960s Blouke found both progressive and traditional elements necessary in building the Open Court program that would enable students to read good literature and begin thinking for themselves. Now, in the 1980s, Bereiter and Scardamalia were realizing that neither progressive nor traditional philosophies of education provided a useful guide to helping students learn to think for themselves. This convergence of perspectives, plus a new infusion of research data, placed Open Court in a position to try again for its ultimate goal. Organizationally, however, it was in trouble.

10. Selling reform by disguise: the move toward the middle (1983–1989)

"There are circumstances in which it is best to package our revolutionary aspirations in harmless-looking exteriors. . . . We should swallow our pride and let [teachers] think we are bland and acceptable. We should fool them and play to their complacent pieties. But we should never for a moment fool ourselves." –André Carus, February 6, 1984

UNDER PRESSURE

IN THE MID-1980s Open Court seemed to face insurmountable opportunities. The 1983 "Nation at Risk" report renewed public concern about dumbed-down education. Blouke felt that the world had made a "sudden turn . . . towards the Open Court basic principles," including the belief that "education is too important to be left to the educators." Research findings were increasingly available that could turn the near-panic into actual improvement in the classroom. Open Court might have been well-placed to profit from the situation, but was itself lacking in money, management, and – for a time – vision.

Most basic was the company's long-standing shortage of capital. Open Court never sold enough textbooks to finance the expensive revisions that states and large school districts required every few years. In the early 1980s the company's annual sales were under $10 million a year, less than half the amount needed to maintain a single program, according to one estimate. As a result Blouke searched for outside investors in 1982–83, 1985–86, and again in 1988–89. At times he seriously considered selling the textbook operation outright.

The company's management situation was almost as dire. Since Howard Webber's arrival at Open Court in 1974, day-to-day direction of the company had increasingly passed out of Blouke's hands. Webber's March 1983 departure was precipitated both by a bitter Carus family dispute and by one of Blouke's searches for outside capital. Management responsibility shifted several times in the ensuing years, as heir-apparent André Carus joined the company and quickly moved up. Early in 1985 he and his father were on increasingly bad terms with André's nominal superior, general manager James Heywood.

In the marketplace, too, Open Court was being backed into a corner. With fewer kids in school there were fewer sales to be made. The small companies Open Court had originally competed with in the phonics market, such as Lippincott and Economy, were either declining or gone, while the large companies were merging with one another at a prodigious rate. Open Court's share of the reading market hovered between 2 and 3 percent, while the big four – Ginn, Houghton, Scott Foresman, and Harcourt Brace Jovanovich – controlled about two-thirds. These textbook giants were imitating Open Court just enough to make their programs look serious – including more phonics in the early grades (although still not well integrated into the rest of the program), and providing more challenging reading material in the later grades. It may have been window dressing, but Jeanne Chall herself attributed a slight rise in scores on the National Assessment of Educational Progress to "an earlier start, more and earlier phonics, harder basal readers grade for grade, more home instruction, more help to those who needed it and the like."

For all these reasons, Blouke was ready for help when he lunched with former Open Court editor Tom Anderson and his partner Gary Marple in Boston on January 18, 1985. Blouke found himself "surprised and impressed" at how Tom had reinvented himself in the seven years since he'd left his editorial position at Open Court. Having worked his way up at Ginn to become Director of Research and Planning, he had then joined Marple (formerly with Arthur D. Little) in the consulting firm Commonwealth Strategies. "They qualify to be among the top people in the United States," Blouke wrote, "and have been used by Scholastic, Ginn, and other major publishers in analyzing the elementary reading and mathematics markets."

MOVING TOWARD THE MIDDLE

The most ominous news didn't surface until Anderson and Marple started consulting for Open Court. Even as the textbook business became less forgiving, Open Court's sales had increased from $4.7 million in 1976 to $6 million in 1981. But the numbers were deceiving. In September 1982, assistant general manager Ed Manfre had dug into the files and discovered that the company's increased sales did not reflect an increasing share of the textbook market. They simply meant that Open Court was selling more workbooks to fewer students.

The company had compromised its anti-workbook principles in 1974 when it included *Headway* workbooks as an essential part of its program. Because workbooks are used up and have to be purchased anew each year, for the first time Open Court sales could increase without the number of customers increasing. No one had been in a position to notice that this was in fact happening.

In addition, Anderson and Marple concluded that Open Court was about to lose its target market and become economically homeless. The phonics segment of the reading market, which the company had inhabited for its entire existence, had almost vanished, they claimed, in the five-year plan they proposed for the company in August 1985. "The segments formerly served by Open Court, Economy, and Lippincott appear to have been shrinking drastically since the late seventies. Lippincott has virtually been driven out of business, Economy has declined to about half its former size, and the biggest basal publishers have added phonics and comprehension to their programs." The big companies could no longer write off any small segment of the textbook market. "By 1985 all mainstream programs emphasize phonics to the extent that it is no longer an issue on which they are vulnerable." Other once-unique features of Open Court's programs, like worthwhile literature and comprehension, "are all being imitated or claimed by the competition."

Now that school enrollment was set to grow again, Anderson and Marple argued that "being or behaving like one of the majors is the way to thrive in the eighties." Veteran Open Court editor Dale Howard reflected on this claim years later. "In a way, Tom sold us a bill of goods. He told Blouke, your problem is you don't have enough warehouse space to hold everything you're going to sell."

As for *Real Math,* the consultants were flummoxed. The program had been created to teach math in the best way possible, without much thought of how it would be sold. They couldn't discern any "segment" of the math market that it could be sold to.

Since Open Court was no longer unique and could not hope to be the cheapest program on the market, the consultants wrote, it would have to distinguish itself in either of two ways. One approach would be to "strengthen its focus," reinforcing ties to current customers and to those using similar programs. In practice this would mean the company should "identify and market to the present customers of Economy and Lippincott, who are most like Open Court's customers in desiring a strong phonics-based reading program, and to the users of the Ginn Language Program, who are most like Open Court's middle-grades customers in placing a high value on composition."

Alternatively, Open Court could "move toward the center" and try to sell to customers "who are at or near the center of the market but who have an interest in or place a higher than average value on the program benefits created by using Open Court's basal programs."

Read in cold blood, these alternatives are hard to tell apart. The targeted customers appear to be the same teachers and administrators, described in different ways. But Anderson and Marple were not just selling vacuum. They were asking the company to improve its attitude. "An adversarial attitude has entered into the thoughts and actions of Open Court personnel that results in a 'we' and 'they' mentality. The 'we' is Open Court, the 'they' is the market. This outlook must be turned around, or Open Court's market will diminish. Most people know who their friends really are and cannot be fooled."

Anderson and Marple recommended that Open Court move toward the center. Its new textbooks should "look more conventional than at present without compromising the program content. . . . the new Open Court program should only look as different as it must be to deliver its educational benefits, rather than looking different at every point so as to draw attention to its unique stance."

André had the difficult task of selling this plan to the group of authors who were already putting together the successor to *Headway, Open Court Reading and Writing* (OCRW). "We will always appeal only to a relatively small minority," he wrote in February 1986. "But to attract even that minority, we have to be *acceptable* to a larger fraction of the market than we are now." In the past Open Court had often relied on strong administrators to choose the program and then to make sure teachers used it properly, as in Rochester and Berkeley (Chapter 7). But teachers' power was growing and such leaders were becoming scarce. As textbooks increasingly were chosen either by committees of untrained volunteers or by all-teacher votes, the books' superficial appearance became increasingly important. If Open Court's materials could not pass the notorious "thumb test" (looking good when a teacher flipped quickly through them), they would never have a chance to be examined more closely.

Open Court had traditionally sold its textbooks by showcasing the results they got for the students. "I'd tell them it was designed for kids," recalls Whyte Ellington, who sold Open Court in North Carolina for eighteen years. "If I saw their eyes light up, then I knew I had them." Now André wanted salespeople to emphasize how Open Court benefited teachers. "Teachers are in control almost everywhere," he wrote, "and if we cannot appear to meet the needs of teachers, we will have no chance of survival in the extremely competitive market we now face. Remember that teachers are not looking to us for enlightenment. They believe that they are educated professionals, and think they need no instruction in how to do their jobs. They do not think a reading program can make much of a difference, except to make life slightly easier or more difficult. They are mostly middle-aged, and have fixed beliefs about what 'works'. . . . We want to go on changing educational practices through published reading programs, and we still think that this is possible. But we are now more aware that we have to give teachers something in return for changing their ways."

RESISTING THE MOVE

Wait a minute, said Carl Bereiter. If the mainstream of the textbook market is so great, why has Open Court been doing better than Lippincott and Economy, which had been the more mainstream publishers in its niche?

Selling on the basis of teacher benefits was perhaps not so very different from Nellie Thomas's "Let the Children Do the Work," or the way in which Bereiter himself had presented the kindergarten program in the early 1970s (Chapter 5). But as an overall corporate orientation he found it inappropriate, even alarming. "Short-term considerations may be dictating a strategy that results in long-term commitment to a centrist, gradualist policy that none of us, authors or publishers, really likes or believes in and that may prove to be a commercial failure as well."

Bereiter insisted that Anderson and Marple were dealing with appearances as if they were realities, while missing the pedagogical point. "Phonics, as taught in the conventional basals, is a travesty. It goes on for years and years, getting into increasingly recondite peculiarities of the English spelling system. It has nothing at all to do with teaching fluent and accurate decoding." As it turned out, mainstream phonics was even more useless than Bereiter thought. A few years later, Linda Cave analyzed for Open Court the phonics elements in major publishers' programs. "None of these programs taught the children to read unknown words by using a consistent decoding strategy. None had direct teaching of sound-symbol correspondences. None offered a true program of phonemic awareness activities. All the programs pulled their phonic elements from the text, *but the instruction was incidental to the reading. The program could be taught without the phonics.*"

Just as it's easier to teach a list of phonics rules than to teach the decoding skills they codify, Bereiter added, "We may expect to see the same thing happening in the teaching of comprehension. It will be converted to (largely false) rules taught as subject matter. And it will have nothing to do with teaching active, strategically-guided reading processes. . . . Converting innovations to subject matter makes it possible to incorporate new elements into a curriculum without changing the basic goals and strategies of the curriculum." That might satisfy mainstream publishers and educators, but Open Court was intent on real change. How could the company possibly disguise that? "When a program is aimed at redressing fundamental deficiencies in the way something is taught, it cannot succeed by catering to those deficiencies. 'Consciousness raising' of some kind is required."

As a business, Open Court had to serve consumers. As a

reform organization, it had to raise their consciousness. Rarely had the two parts of its mission seemed so incompatible. Dale Howard reflects that he and other old-timers in the company were ill-positioned to distinguish between the valid and invalid parts of Marple's and Anderson's plan. Open Court had long set itself apart from and above companies driven exclusively by marketing considerations. As Howard Webber wrote in Open Court's "Bulletin" in 1976, "It is *conviction* that has led Open Court to where it is, not market research." In an academic metaphor, its people had been the liberal-arts students looking down on the business school. But now that they needed business-school expertise, they were unable to judge it critically. It was all or nothing. As Dale Howard recalls, "We didn't understand that you can have this knowledge without its corrupting you."

As an alternative to moving toward the center of the market, Bereiter proposed a "niche-creating strategy" which would face the fact that new things need to be taught in new ways. Teachers would be asked to make "a dramatic change in orientation – away from teaching content and exercising skills and toward teaching skills and giving children more of the responsibility for digging out the content, away from 'directing' the reading and writing processes and toward teaching the skills needed for self-direction." What large publisher would try to mimic that?

André stood fast on the conventional marketing wisdom that niche markets can only be discovered, not created. Even the current Open Court program, he said, was not conservative but "quite radical" by market standards. "Primitive as you may now find them, Workshop and the Composition Cycle have probably had a greater effect in getting teachers to allow and encourage more student-directed behaviors than any other influence now operating on the elementary market. . . . You researchers may have trouble noticing these differences, but school people do not. Even the present Open Court program is definitely 'noticed' as being something very different."

André was the boss by now, and he won this battle – although it might not have mattered if the Caruses' search for outside capital had not finally borne fruit: in 1986 the Bingham family of Louisville invested $3.5 million in Open Court and in 1989 they made another $5 million available, enough to make possible the publication of *Open Court Reading and Writing* in 1989. Mary Bingham, a long-time supporter of the Council for Basic Education, said, "I feel that my investment in Open Court is the most effective contribution I can make toward solving the national literacy problem."

It's important to see the argument for what it was – a principled disagreement, not a contest between purity on one side and corruption on the other. Both parties understood the nuances of each other's position. Bereiter agreed that some compromises were necessary in order to crack the education culture. As Bereiter acknowledged later that year in correspondence, those who author textbooks "are forced to make concessions to the prevailing practices. The concessions involve among other things providing some minimum of seatwork exercises," aka worksheets or dittos – which, he noted, have no pedagogical justification from *any* point of view, but are included simply "to satisfy teachers' beliefs in their efficacy and teachers' reliance on routinized seatwork to free up time."

And André agreed that not all compromises were acceptable. In June 1986 he advised the authors of his determination *not* to make certain concessions to the market. "As you know, even our best and most cooperative customers are forever pestering us about wanting comprehension questions, esp. in HIJ [4th–6th grades], where they are not printed in the readers. (There are lots of questions in the [teachers'] guides . . . . But this does not seem to be enough. They want something called 'written' comprehension, and we have actually been made to reproduce those questions from the guides as dittos as a condition for being adopted in several districts.) And if there is a clear message from the market research (backed up – loudly – by our sales force), it is that comprehension questions in some form or another are about as basic as racial balance in the readers. Such things are conditions for even being considered. . . . Nonetheless, we are determined to resist as far as resistance is possible."

FAILING THE TEST

Thumb-testers had no trouble spotting Open Court's move

toward the middle. Its bold color and splashy graphics made *Open Court Reading and Writing* seem much more like a consumer product than *Headway* had been. Those who examined it more closely found that some former Open Court hallmarks, like Jerry Lebo's "hot teaching" (Chapter 5), were missing. But each skill being taught was labeled so that teachers couldn't miss it.

The new strategy called for a major change in the work of the company's sales force. Anderson and Marple postulated that Open Court had to emerge from its vanishing niche and try to win away the big companies' customers. At the same time salespeople were once more asked to lay more emphasis on literature and comprehension, and less on phonics, than they were accustomed to doing. "Predictably," recalls then sales manager Dick Rogers, "the mainstreaming changes were welcomed by some of the sales force – primarily those brought in from other publishing companies to help bring Open Court into the big leagues – and were resisted by others – primarily the 'evangelicals' in the field force who had long been associated with the program." Some of the latter group quit; a few even wondered if Anderson was trying to destroy the company with bad counsel. In retrospect, says André Carus, "Tom underestimated the strength of the sales culture."

Marple and Anderson's strategy could only be vindicated by *OCRW*'s sales. Sales did rise significantly, doubling from $8.4 million in 1984 to $17.2 million in 1989 – but they fell well short of the $22.5 million the company had counted on. By summer, when it was clear that sales would fall $5 million short, more than one-third of the company's employees were let go. As if to pound the point home, just as *Open Court Reading and Writing* was garnering disappointing results, *Real Math,* with its much less compromising façade, had begun to exceed expectations.

According to sales veteran Karen Hansill, some old customers saw *OCRW* as watered down. But it still puzzled new customers with unique Open Court jargon like "word lines" and "workshop." Looking superficially more like conventional publishers had not worked, Carl Bereiter concluded afterwards. "The effect on naive evaluators . . . is that Open Court materials shift from being judged unacceptable to being judged acceptable but not quite as good as competing materials; hence, still no sale."

FINDING A BALANCE

In April 1990, two all-day company meetings buried the Anderson-Marple strategy. "We now believe," André wrote, "that change is coming, and that it will be fundamental. As a result, we believe that we can come out of the closet and be frank about our leadership role, about being different and better – instead of having to hide that mission under an apparent blandness of program content and appearance." An early draft of the company's 1990–95 strategic plan saw the reading market as being segmented into status quo and reforming ("leadership") districts. Open Court would sell to the reforming districts.

The drastic nature of this reversal did not escape company staff. Members of the Field Advisory Board welcomed it but wondered "how it fits with our attempts, over the last five years, to move closer to the mainstream." In substance it directly contradicted what Anderson and Marple had said in 1985. In style, however, the new plan still owed something to the consultants. "Being more customer oriented has clearly helped us. So have a lot of other things that have brought us out of our 'niche,' such as stressing other things than phonics, stressing K-6 [as opposed to K-3 or K-1], appearing more friendly and less snobbish, etc." Accordingly the move toward the middle, although now viewed as a mistake, had not been a dead end in terms of marketing. Open Court would "pursue the leadership strategy in reading and math, without losing the new-found customer-orientation and friendliness."

In retrospect, André describes the company's reorientation rhetoric as "whistling in the dark." Financially, the move toward the middle had been a disaster. The company teetered on the edge of bankruptcy even as it prepared to rewrite its bread-and-butter program from scratch for the second time in less than a decade. (*OCRW* had been expected to have a ten-year life.) "We essentially had one more chance."

But before that, Open Court had to take *OCRW* into the fiery furnace of a California textbook adoption battle – a battle that would confirm André's statement that any disagreements within the company paled by comparison with how much it differed from the rest of the textbook industry.

11. Counterfeit reform (1985–1988)

"It is maddening to be rejected in the name of the very ideals we have for so long been fighting for." – Blouke Carus, November 17, 1988

STATE ADOPTIONS: REFORM FROM THE TOP DOWN?

TEXTBOOK PUBLISHERS DO not operate in a free market. Their customers, whether individual teachers or local school districts, cannot always buy any textbook they choose. In the mid-1980s, twenty-two state departments of education, most in the South and West, listed acceptable textbooks from which schools could select – "adopting" them, in the industry's jargon. Usually the constraint was financial, with state funds being available only for listed books; occasionally it was legal.

State adoptions were originally intended to make sure schools got quantity discounts on quality textbooks, leading to a uniform statewide curriculum. As the Sunbelt states grew in population in the 1970s, state adoptions came to be seen as a way to control textbooks' content nationwide. California, for instance, with about 12 percent of the U.S. textbook market, was big enough to be influential but not big enough to justify a special edition sold only there. Publishers would therefore go out of their way to do what California wanted, and anyone who could affect California adoption decisions gained power over what textbooks would be available in other states as well. Advocates of fundamentalism, feminism, racial diversity, and other causes began to descend on state adoption panels to argue that textbooks should reflect their points of view.

Being adopted was an essential preliminary to selling (a "hunting license"), but it did not guarantee a publisher success. And the adoption process was more arduous than selling to individual school districts (as publishers could in other parts of the U.S.). Even a small state enjoys more bargaining power than a single school district. Adoption states could and did insist on "entertainment, bogus consulting contracts, contributions to political campaigns, subsidized trips, gifts, 'free' in-service training contracts, or 'free' materials," as Harriet Tyson wrote on behalf of the Council for Basic Education in February 1989. The adoption states could also require more educationally defensible measures like durability standards for books and learner-verification studies. Thus state adoptions favored the larger and better-capitalized firms, while posing a harsh dilemma to smaller fry like Open Court.

Open Court's double identity made it ambivalent about state adoptions. From a business point of view, they demanded extra resources without guaranteeing additional sales, although adoption in California could serve as a badge of merit elsewhere. Company sales figures for 1987 and 1988 show that the company got just over half of its reading revenue from "open" territories, where it could target innovative or otherwise promising districts one at a time, with less up-front expenditure of time and money.

From a reform point of view, state adoptions seemed to promise Open Court the same leverage they offered other advocates. But adoptions were not about reform. As author Paul Goldstein (*Changing the American Schoolbook: Law, Politics, and Technology*) was quoted in *Education Week* in 1984, educators tend to adopt materials "that are very much like those already in use, with just enough surface differences to give the impression of change and to make the selection process appear worthwhile. The entire thrust of the selection process is to preserve the status quo."

At the state level, adoptions preserve the status quo in at least three ways:

* Adopting for all grades at once. As University of Chicago education professor Zalman Usiskin wrote to Blouke in 1987, "A process in which adoption of textbooks for all years K-6 or K-8 is made simultaneously makes it impossible for substantial change to be considered. After all, if a new grade 6 is to follow old grades 1–5, then it can't require knowledge much different than that acquired in the old curriculum. Districts adopting your [Open Court's] materials are well advised to introduce them one year at a time. . . . Adoptions almost universally assume the curriculum will not change enough to make a difference."

* Adopting many different textbooks at once. Since a long list of adopted materials usually includes at least one familiar and mediocre offering, it allows state officials to point with pride to the excellent textbooks on their list, while local schools continue with their routine. *Real Math* author Stephen Willoughby compared a state making multiple textbook adoptions to a Board of Health refusing to approve any cancer treatments for use until several companies came up with one. "Drug companies would certainly not try to be first to produce such a drug if they realized they could get no return on their investment until four other companies had followed their lead."

* Combining high-minded statements of purpose with routine or fad-driven implementation. Routine ruled in 1981 in West Virginia. The state approved all the mathematics textbooks submitted, with the exception of *Real Math*. At the time West Virginia had no math supervisor and provided no formal grounds for the rejection. Informally it appeared that the program was seen as just too different – among other things, the state adoption committee claimed that it "would require extensive retraining of teachers." The California math and reading adoptions of the late 1980s, discussed below, were more sophisticated, in that state education officials conveyed the impression of change to the media while catering to instructional fads and causing little or no actual disturbance to the education culture.

As in every aspect of the education culture, one should avoid over-intellectualizing what is often the result of simple ignorance and inertia. When Mary Courtland and colleagues studied Indiana's 1982 reading adoption, they found that the reviewers, mostly teachers, relied primarily on their personal teaching experience. "Theoretical viewpoints regarding the teaching process and recent educational research were almost never mentioned as factors influencing their decisions," nor were school districts' reading objectives. Of course, the Indiana reviewers had neither the time nor the training to evaluate textbooks in an intellectually serious way. Many, for instance, "had time only to 'flip through' some of the texts to gain a general impression of the content."

Beginning in the 1980s, state adoptions combined with the nationwide pressure for higher standards may actually have made textbooks worse. Educators' response to the pressure was not creative but mechanical. They used state adoption procedures, as Tyson wrote in 1988, "to specify, in excruciating detail, all the facts, terms, and topics that must be included in the textbooks they are willing to buy," so that the books would match up with standardized test questions. "Thus the *de facto* national curriculum is a thin stream of staccato prose winding through an excessive number of pictures, boxes, and charts." *Christian Science Monitor* education writer Robert Marquand found that Florida and Wisconsin were each mandating 1,000 references in certain textbooks. Tyson concluded that "State regulatory power over textbooks has generally been a negative influence on textbook quality."

Sometimes state adoptions were absurd to the point of hilarity, as when the Commonwealth of Virginia in 1988 rejected Open Court because the company had supposedly offered inadequate decoding strategies and weak literature, while failing to teach comprehension strategies. These charges were implausible at best. But Virginia also criticized Open Court for failing to meet learning standards for seventh and eighth grades – for which the company had never produced a reading program at all! The evaluation forms on which these statements were based proved to be mysteriously unavailable.

State power was no joke for Open Court in California in the late 1980s. Unlike many adoption states, California had over the years gone to great lengths to formalize and professionalize its procedures. And on this occasion, a seemingly serious reformer named Bill Honig presided over successive California adoptions for mathematics and language arts. Open Court was able to make both adoption lists, a Pyrrhic victory given the cost in money and time. But in each case the state's high-minded reform statements were subverted in broad daylight, with Honig's enthusiastic approval.

CALIFORNIA MATH

In the 1985–86 mathematics adoption, California played the part of the teacher who finds out who threw the spitwad but keeps the whole class in from recess anyway. The state's March 1985 guidelines for math textbooks, known as the "Framework," called for California students to understand math concepts and skills, not just learn by rote. The students were to have a greater variety of experiences with numbers than just performing pen-and-pencil operations, and they were to apply their skills to solve problems. California was echoing the NCTM's 1980 *Agenda for Action,* which in turn reflected the principles on which *Real Math* had been built in the 1970s.

"The California Math Framework of 1985 cannot be praised too highly," Blouke told the American Educational Research Association. "I urge everyone to read it; it may not read like a Dick Francis novel, but for anyone interested in the survival and growth of this country's economy and technology, and expanding opportunities for all children, this document makes bedside reading."

The Framework was only the beginning of a bureaucratic Pilgrim's Progress for publishers. They would submit their textbooks, and volunteer educators serving on three separate Instructional Materials Evaluation Panels measured the books against the Framework. The IMEPs' judgments were then forwarded to a Subject Matter Committee, which made recommendations to the Curriculum Development and Supplemental Materials Commission, which in turn made recommendations to the state Board of Education, which issued the final list of adopted textbooks.

This pilgrimage began with a fundamental confusion. On one hand, the 1985 Framework implied an absolute standard when it said the state would adopt only textbooks that promoted understanding and problem solving, and not rote memorization. On the other hand, state law implied a relative standard when it said that the state would adopt at least five textbooks. What if fewer than five measured up? Would California adopt only those books that satisfied its guidelines? Or would it adopt whichever five came closest?

In 1986, fourteen publishers submitted math textbooks. Each of the three IMEPs gave top rank to Open Court's *Real Math* as the textbook series best meeting the Framework. The ambiguity in state standards still might have languished in obscurity, except that the Mathematics Subject Matter Committee decided to take the Framework seriously.

"Few of the submitted materials even moderately matched the Framework," the committee reported on September 24, and it refused to recommend as many as five of them because "the books that would be recommended failed to demonstrate an adequate match with the Framework and [recommending them] would communicate to the publishing industry and the education profession that the standards set forth in the Framework were, in actuality, of little importance." (More to the point educationally, such an action would have perpetuated the status quo in which, for instance, 43 percent of California sixth-graders believed that 143.5 = 143 1/5.) By a 5-1 vote, the Mathematics Subject Matter Committee recommended that the state adopt *only* Open Court's *Real Math* for grades K-8, while giving seven other publishers two years to rewrite and resubmit their programs.

The Curriculum Development and Supplemental Materials Commission took only two days to reject this recommendation and turn Open Court's stunning victory into an even more stunning defeat. The Curriculum Commission made the unprecedented proposal, which the state board of education approved, that the state reject *all* the submitted textbooks and give their publishers one year to rewrite and resubmit them.

It is difficult to imagine any legal action California could have taken that would have been more destructive to the goals stated in its Framework. Not only had the state rejected the judgment of the only people who had actually examined the books in question, it had punished all publishers alike regardless of merit. "In the name of improving education," wrote *Real Math* author Steve Willoughby, "textbook publishers were condemned as a group for not doing what one of them had actually done. And publishers were discouraged from producing better textbooks when they saw the good tarred with the same brush as the mediocre."

Even more destructively, by allowing just one year to revise, California treated basic textbook concepts on a par with illustrations or typography – as if they could be intelligently altered in a short time. No textbook can be rethought from first principles, rewritten, tried out in classrooms, and revised, all in just one year. As the University of Chicago's Zalman Usiskin noted, "The events of the California adoption increase the likelihood that untested materials will be perpetrated on the children of California; indeed, they ensure it."

Had there been no other oddities in the state's procedure, this draconian time limit alone signaled that California had given up on its attempt to bring about reform through the adoption process. A second indication was that the state Department of Education set up new rules, much sketchier than the original Framework, under which an Extended Mathematics Adoption Committee member would negotiate individually with publishers. "There were no rules," says Blouke. "It was strictly ad hoc." (*Real Math* was adopted under this procedure early in 1987.)

"All publishers have had two years to develop programs to meet the specifications of the California framework," Blouke wrote indignantly to the California board. "Obviously many of the publishers did not pay much attention to the framework, so that postponing the decision another year (or more) rewards those publishers for thinking they did not have to make significant changes, and penalizes Open Court for having the 15 years of foresight for committing the company, finding the best authors, performing extensive and sequential field testing, and committing more than a decade of investment without any indication of financial viability."

The notion that a state adoption might improve mathematics education lay in tatters, but nobody noticed. Media accounts followed the lead of Honig's office, which described the wholesale rejection as a way of insisting on higher standards. Math author Marilyn Burns was one of many journalists who fell for it, writing in the January 1987 issue of *Learning* magazine that "the state is holding out for the best and refusing to accept less."

California's 1985 Framework had called for a revolution in American elementary math teaching (a revolution which has yet to occur, by the way, according to the findings of the Third International Math and Science Study). Thanks to the state's contradictory mandates and bizarre implementation procedure, the education culture absorbed the impact and emerged unscathed. The one member of the Subject Matter Committee who voted against recommending only *Real Math* cited the fact that a number of California districts had *already* themselves "pre-adopted" other textbooks.

CALIFORNIA READING

Words and deeds diverged even further in the next two years. California's *English-Language Arts Framework,* issued in 1987, once more seemed promising to Blouke, compared to the status-quo mindsets in other states. In some ways the Framework paralleled Open Court. It called for students to read good literature and "discover the best that human beings have thought, written, and spoken"; to do so via a program that integrated reading, writing, listening, and speaking; and not to depend on rote activities or tests for assessment.

But this Framework too harbored errors and ambiguities. Most strangely, it recommended "a phonics program taught in meaningful contexts, kept simple, and completed in the early grades" as opposed to "an intensive phonics program extending into the middle and even upper grades." The distinction makes no sense. Open Court's intensive phonics program was finished before the end of first grade, whereas mainstream publishers dribbled out rules for years. Nor can sound-spelling correspondences always be taught in "meaningful contexts," that is, using texts with inherent interest or literary value. Teaching any skill requires repetition, and few great works of literature concentrate on long "e." Reading practice is to reading as basketball practice is to basketball, providing in both cases that the learners understand the point of the practice. (How long would a basketball coach last who insisted that dribbling be taught only "in meaningful contexts," i.e. during games?)

Even more ominously, the Framework waffled on the crucial question of skills. On the one hand, it cited the 1985 research synthesis *Becoming a Nation of Readers*. On the other hand, nowhere did the Framework acknowledge that volume's crucial message – that there should be no dichotomy between "teaching for skills" and "teaching for meaning," because students need both. Instead the Framework affirmed Frank Smith's unsupported assertion that "Children learn to read by reading."

So the company was in trouble even before the evaluations began. Then things got worse. Some members of the IMEPs rejected Open Court because it taught skills (which the authors of *Open Court Reading and Writing* had obligingly labeled as such, as part of the company's attempt to move toward the middle of the market). But this reason for rejection contradicted most educational research, so other panels tried to find less embarrassing reasons to reject Open Court – by claiming that it did not integrate reading, writing, listening, and speaking, or that it had omitted or watered down good literature. The fact that these claims were transparently false did not prevent them from almost succeeding.

"The quality of literature is diminished at the beginning levels [of Open Court] because stories which appear in the student texts are clearly written to illustrate phonetic principles," complained the members of one Instructional Materials Evaluation Panel. "There is no evidence of themes in student literature until second grade. . . . This practice constitutes phonetic based, not literature-based instruction." Another panel seemed confused, first stating that *Open Court Reading and Writing* "exemplifies all the features of an effective integrated language arts program described in the Framework," but concluded nevertheless that it should not be adopted! Another claimed, falsely, that *OCRW* had omitted parts of "The Tale of Peter Rabbit" and omitted the phrase "I think I can, I think I can" from "The Little Engine That Could."

All three panels assumed that "skills" and "meaning" were opposed, and recommended that California not adopt *OCRW.*

At July hearings before the Curriculum Development and Supplemental Materials Commission, Jean Osborn of the University of Illinois Center for the Study of Reading identified the dubious basis of the IMEPs' criticisms: "'Becoming a Nation of Readers' recommends that systematic phonics instruction be an important part of a beginning reading program, and further-more that children must practice in the stories they read the sound/symbol relationships they are learning. For this to happen, stories must contain words that the students know how to figure out (decode). . . . The panels' comments about the quality of lit-erature in the beginning levels of this program imply that there is great literature that reflects the beginning word recognition instruction of any given reading program. This is not often the case. Of primary importance is that children read stories that enable them to practice what they are learning and to become successful at reading."

An understandably bewildered André Carus reminded the commission, "For 25 years, we have stood firm against pressure to dilute our reader selections or apply readability formulas to them – *especially* at grades 1 to 3. So naturally we're amazed that California, which said it wanted literature, is accusing us of exact-ly the things we've been fighting against all these years. It's as if someone told Jesse Jackson he was not concerned enough about the poor."

The testimony had little effect. The Curriculum Development and Supplemental Materials Commission adopted *Open Court Reading and Writing* only for grades 3–6. That amounted to a death sentence, since most of the company's revenues came in the earlier grades, and few districts would switch programs at third grade. Now only the California Board of Education itself stood between the company and oblivion.

DAVID AND GOLIATH

What had been difficult for Open Court now began to approach the impossible, costing enormous amounts of time – André spent

most of the summer of 1988 in California rather than in his office
– and unaffordable sums of money spent on public relations,
lawyers, and lobbyists. The Caruses mobilized a network of school
reformers, academics, journalists, and teachers in a final effort to
persuade the state Board of Education to overrule the
Commission. "Open Court has gone out onto a limb," Blouke
wrote to cultural-literacy advocate E.D. Hirsch August 3, "and if
the mainstream publishers see that rhetoric and appearances are
enough while reality lags comfortably behind, they will never follow us out onto that limb.

"Open Court has unequivocally hitched its cart to cultural literacy; it is what I started the reading program for 26 years ago,
and the contrast between our readers [with which he acknowledged he was not completely happy] and the others is still very
great. We have invested many millions of dollars in our new reading program – dangerously many, in the view of our banks – and
if we are seen to fail, it will not only discourage the mainstream
companies from imitating us, it will seriously threaten Open
Court's ability to even go on existing for others to imitate."

To his sales staff Blouke described the impending battle as
David vs. Goliath, and indeed it seemed likely that the board of
education would follow the lower panels' recommendations. In a
July 27 press release, Superintendent of Public Instruction Honig
endorsed them, saying, "These recommendations give us books
with *real* literature – with real values and ideas – not soft, shallow
children's stories." In a widely circulated newspaper column,
Honig was quoted as describing André Carus as "a disgruntled
person who's not going to get his books adopted" and Open
Court as having provided "watered-down literature."

E.D. Hirsch himself conclusively refuted these statements by
comparing the various textbook series' late first-grade readers. He
simply counted the number of "well-known fables and fairy tales,
nursery rhymes, and non-fiction about things that can be said to
be part of our 'cultural heritage'" in each publisher's offerings.
Macmillan had two such items out of 25 in its reader, Scott
Foresman four, Heath three, McGraw-Hill one, Holt one, and

Houghton Mifflin none. All had been recommended for adoption.

Open Court presented a different picture in the hardbound reader for the second semester of first grade. This book, Hirsch noted, "contains 'The Fox and the Grapes,' 'The House that Jack Built,' 'The Three Bears,' 'The Lion and the Mouse,' 'The Little Engine That Could,' 'The Hare and the Tortoise,' 'The Three Billy Goats Gruff,' 'The Wolf in Sheep's Clothing,' 'The Gingerbread Boy,' the Aesop fable 'The Silkworm and the Spider,' 'The Itsy, Bitsy Spider,' 'Dick Whittington and His Cat,' 'Pussy-Cat, Pussy-Cat,' two fables by Leo Tolstoy ('The Plum Pit' and 'The Happy Tailor'), and two non-fiction articles about things everyone ought to know: 'Jane Goodall' and 'Wilbur and Orville'" – a total of 17 items out of 33, or just over half the reader, and more than all the other series combined. But the Curriculum Commission had refused to adopt it!

The company prepared page-by-page analyses demonstrating that Honig's "soft, shallow children's stories" actually appeared, not in Open Court, but in the series recommended for adoption. For instance, Open Court used the modern classic "Strange Bumps" by Arnold Lobel verbatim in *Rainbow Bridge,* its last first-grade reader. The story tells about a young owl afraid to go to sleep because of the strange bumps (made by his feet) in the covers at the foot of his bed. Lobel's original reads, "Owl lifted up the blanket. He looked down into the bed. All he could see was darkness. Owl tried to sleep, but he could not. 'What if those two strange bumps grow bigger and bigger while I am asleep?' said Owl. 'That would not be pleasant.'" In contrast, McGraw-Hill's many small adaptations drained the color from the passage: "Owl looked under the blanket. He looked down into the bed. It was dark. Owl wanted to get some rest, but he could not. 'Those strange bumps might get big when I am sleeping,' said Owl. 'That would not be nice.'"

Not only was the vocabulary watered down – "nice" for "pleasant," likely a concession to readability formulas – but it was changed for no perceptible reason other than to create repetition

("looked under" for "lifted up"). The style had also been dena-
tured, replacing the author's memorably idiosyncratic "All he
could see was darkness" with "It was dark." And the phrase "What
if . . . grow bigger and bigger" was inexplicably turned into the
awkward "might get big." The adaptation even altered the meaning of one sentence by substituting "wanted to get some rest" for
"tried to sleep."

At least the main idea of Lobel's story survived cheapening.
Heath's version of Rachel Isadora's "Willaby" omitted much of the
context *OCRW* retained, establishing the main character's love of
drawing. Scott Foresman's excerpt from Patricia MacLachlan's
"Through Grandpa's Eyes" made the story shorter, blander, and
harder to follow by omitting full pages of colorful examples
included in the *OCRW* version. McGraw-Hill rendered Aesop's
fable about the hare and the tortoise all but incomprehensible
even to those who already knew the story. In short, Open Court
concluded, "The recommended programs contain far fewer classical selections in readers, and far fewer of the selections in
California's own list of recommended readings. Where modern
children's classics are included, they are abridged, edited, and
simplified much more than in Open Court's readers."

More technical but equally dubious was the IMEPs' claim that
Open Court had failed to integrate listening, speaking, reading,
and writing as the Framework required. As *OCRW* author Valerie
Anderson explained in September 1988 testimony before the
California Board of Education, "The chief method of meaningful-
ly integrating all of these language arts in *Open Court Reading and
Writing* is classroom discussion that is student-centered and student directed. This form of discussion occurs before, during, and
after both reading and writing." How could the evaluation panels
have missed this? Anderson tactfully suggested that Open Court
might have been guilty of subtlety. "The evaluators may not have
seen this in *Open Court Reading and Writing,* because these four
aspects of language experience are not separately labeled in the
program and hence are not quickly visible. In the programs that
are recommended for across-the-board approval, they are so
labeled."

Similarly, she argued, *OCRW* matched the Framework's call for textbooks to help students learn how to construct their own meaning. "One quick test to apply to demonstrate this is to look at the number of questions asked by the teacher versus the number of opportunities for the students to ask their own questions and make their own comments. Some of the recommended programs have as many as 40 teacher-given 'comprehension' questions per story." By contrast, *OCRW* is "rich in opportunities for the children's own experiences, ideas, and questions, no lesson with more than four teacher-directed questions, and then only to [make] important points that integrate meaning."

After the September hearing at which these and other points were made, the state board reversed the commission's recommendation and adopted *OCRW* in full. But even this victory could be attributed as much to the company's desperate political mobilization as to the merit of its books. As Harriet Tyson put it afterwards, "Whether one views the Board's last actions as an attempt to remedy mistakes in the prior selection process, or as capitulation to political forces, or both, the publishers have learned that the process can be manipulated after the fact. . . . [encouraging] publishers to invest more heavily in the political process than in the careful development of solid instructional materials."

Why had Honig and his minions found it necessary to go out of their way to trash Open Court? The University of Illinois' Richard Anderson thought he knew.

"There is a pattern among the rejected programs: All of them have a reputation for intensive phonics instruction in the lower grades. Educational research in the United States has consistently shown that children make more progress in reading, on the average, when they receive systematic phonics instruction in the early grades. Why, then were programs known for strong phonics recommended for rejection, especially since the Framework endorses phonics instruction? My hunch is that the main reason is the changing winds of ideological fashion. Something called the 'whole language' movement has an enthusiastic following in California reading circles. Much about this movement is positive; it stands for genuine literature, integrating reading and writing, and natural approaches to teaching children to read. However, the most zealous proponents of 'whole language' are as noteworthy for what they are against as what they are for. They absolutely proscribe 'teaching skills in isolation,' which in their minds rules out traditional, systematic approaches to phonics."

Having labored through voluminous forms and interminable hearings, the largest state's adoption process had brought forth a mouse. While claiming to reject dumbed-down textbooks, California adopted them in the name of the latest instructional fad.

12. Whole Language and CYS (1987–1996)

"What Blouke and Marianne Carus have developed, in the past thirty years, on the basis of the old Open Court and their family traditions, is a unique capability to package high literacy in a variety of forms for existing and new consumer groups. This is our core competence, our main competitive strength . . . . the company has repackaged some relatively inaccessible portions of high literacy (educational research, children's literature, top artists and illustrators) for larger consumer groups than had previously had access to it (well-meaning but ill-prepared teachers, educated but unliterary parents)." – André Carus, May 4, 1993

WHOLE LANGUAGE

IN PLANNING THE ill-fated "move toward the middle," Open Court consultants Anderson and Marple managed to miss the big change in the textbook market. By the late 1980s Open Court had indeed lost – not its phonics niche, as the consultants had predicted, but something almost as valuable – its monopoly on zealots. For years company salespeople had faced apathetic teachers, technocratic administrators, and education-school professors devoted to the status quo. Enthusiasts, if any, tended to be on Open Court's side. As late as April 1987, André could write, "One thing we have that our competitors generally lack is a group of very enthusiastic users."

But now the company faced zealous converts to the whole-language gospel. These teachers believed that reading could be learned as easily as talking; that therefore teachers should immerse children in good literature; that the teaching of particular skills was rarely if ever a good idea; that doing so in reading groups separated by ability was worse; that children should be

evaluated positively and by many measures, rarely if ever by formal testing; and – at the extreme – that basal textbooks were not
only unnecessary but an insult to teachers' professionalism.
"When it first started to come in," recalls Whyte Ellington of
North Carolina, "I said to my friends, 'You gotta be kidding.' They
were sure they had found the Holy Grail."

"How anyone could dream up the idea that phonics and other
beginning reading skills are not needed is totally beyond my comprehension!" Blouke wrote to sympathetic academic Patrick Groff
of San Diego State University in the spring of 1989. "This nut is
harder to crack than I would ever have imagined." He dismissed
whole language as "the latest reincarnation of progressive education, anti-phonics, anti-skills, and such movements." Later on he
changed tack, advising a journalist that the whole-language movement was "so powerful it is not worth fighting from our point of
view," and even argued that Open Court should be considered as
"the original whole language program."

No such luck. Despite some overlap, Open Court and whole
language had grown from different roots. Open Court represented a practical engineer's attempt to raise school standards; whole
language was in large part a grass-roots reaction *against* any
attempt to raise school standards. As Jerry Lebo had already
observed, "No one sees that Open Court really incorporates the
best elements of Whole Language, and at the same time provides
insurance against its potential problems." And so the company's
costly California adoption victory yielded few spoils. Open Court
had just 2.6 percent of the first-grade basal reading market in
California at the beginning of the '90s, well below its average of
4.2 percent in adoption states and 5.9 percent in open territories.

As intellectual platforms, whole language and Open Court
agreed on some important points – support for good literature,
opposition to tracking, rejection of readability formulas, and a
desire to evaluate students' progress in many ways (especially by
direct feedback) rather than simply by testing. But their philosophical and political roots set the two well apart. "Some critical
theorists advocating whole language oppose traditional reading

instruction, asserting that it is a tool of the ruling classes to oppress the underclasses, a mechanism for assuring the continuation of the class structure that now exists in America," wrote Michael Pressley and Joan Rankin in *Learning Disabilities Practice* in 1994. "Phonics, basal reading programs, and explicit forms of teaching in general are presented as instruments of capitalists that are used to fill the minds of the disenfranchised with the ideas traditionally supported by the favored groups in American society." Blouke of course had long seen things the other way around – that the schools' failure to teach reading effectively would shut the disenfranchised out of society more permanently than any propaganda ever could.

In any case, whole language was not primarily an intellectual or political platform. It was about feeling good. It represented a resurgence of Romantic Rousseauian fervor in education, a style that, again, fitted poorly with Open Court. Former English teacher Elizabeth New Weld put whole language in parable form for the spring 1990 issue of the *Boston Globe*'s "Young Reader" newsletter:

"Once upon a time, a teacher . . . . filled her classroom with beautiful books – great, big stand-up books for little children; picture books; classic tales; poems for older ones. She read to them; they read to her and to each other. The children shared reading. If someone didn't know the word, the others helped. They didn't know they were learning about language, about reading. . . . When they studied science, she would ask: 'What do you think you'll see when we visit the pond?' . . . When they came back they checked out what they had found against what they had predicted. Then they got used to taking charge of what they learned. . . . When they began to write their stories down, they just wrote the words as best they could, sometimes inventing the spelling. Eventually, through trial and error, they learned to spell the words the way everyone else does and to make the grammar come out right. She didn't test them with standardized tests. She collected their work all year long . . . and made a portfolio. . . . The teachers all gently put aside their basal readers (textbooks that use only

parts of stories) in favor of whole children's books, whole language. . . . [They] liked the idea of taking charge of their classrooms again."

Weld's parable showcased some accepted pedagogic techniques (having books around, reading them aloud, previewing
new experiences and readings) and mixed them with faddish
notions and contradictions (both teacher and students are said to
be "taking charge"). Through the Karo-syrup prose a steely
dogma can be glimpsed: not only must children learn skills by
trial and error, it's strangely important that they not *know* that
they're learning.

To Jeanne Chall this anti-intellectual dogma was all too familiar. "The view in the 1920s was that concentrating on the reading
of interesting stories (with little or no teaching of the forms and
sounds of words) will result in better reading comprehension,"
she wrote in 1991. Back then it had been fashionable to think
"that this procedure will result in lifetime reading, while learning
phonics is dull and dreary and discourages the development of
lifelong reading. Although the research of the past 80 years has
refuted these claims, they remain. And if they are relinquished for
a period, they return as new discoveries, under new labels."

Why this eternal return? "These conceptions promise a quick
and easy solution to reading problems – i.e., reading without
tears, reading full of joy. . . . Whole language, in particular, seems
to say that a good heart goes a long way, and the less teaching, the
better teaching. It fears rote learning more than no learning."

GOING TO EXTREMES

Not all whole-language teachers went all the way. The movement's
leaders were often ahead of its followers. In 1988, Kenneth
Goodman, Patrick Shannon, Yvonne Freeman, and Sharon
Murphy wrote an entire book dissecting and dismissing mainstream basal readers – defined as "a sequential, all-inclusive set of
instructional materials [that] can teach all children to read *regardless of teacher competence* and *regardless of learner differences*." The
authors criticized basal adaptations of children's literature in
terms that echoed Open Court, even as they ignored the compa-

ny's inconvenient existence. "The claims of basal publishers that they draw on the available rich literature for children is certainly true. But it is also true that pupils will rarely meet the language of any children's author in a pure and unadapted form."

The authors went on to make the less plausible assertion that "Basals are either de-emphasized or eliminated altogether" in whole-language schools and classrooms. But it seems that few teachers or schools in fact threw their textbooks away. Some Open Court teachers even described themselves as whole-language advocates. According to the company's 1991 strategic plan, "Traditional practices survive (sometimes with different names) beneath the rhetoric. The vast majority of teachers still depend on teachers' guides for the curriculum, still depend on workbooks and worksheets for classroom management, and still focus attention on the hardbound basal textbook as the primary criterion for adopting a program."

A first-grade teacher from Houston, apparently ignorant of Open Court's textbooks, wrote to the company's *Ladybug* magazine, "Whole language teachers love your kind of stuff. We are the folks teaching from *real* books, songs & poems. We choose not to use the 'Basal reader.' This could be a whole new area of marketing for you."

Blouke agreed. The company played up its points of agreement with whole language. Open Court's Marsha Roit identified as the "heart" of whole language the belief – held by Open Court since its inception – that "all of the language arts should be integrated." Among the sound teaching principles she found embodied both in whole language and in Open Court: "children come to school with an emerging knowledge of reading and writing; children should be read to regularly; children should read quality literature; children should engage in real reading and writing everyday; children should be encouraged to learn in a risk-free environment; children need to learn in an environment that takes advantage of the social nature of literacy."

Another company promotion cut to the chase: "If you like whole language, but want to be sure that your students will learn to read, Open Court Reading and Writing is your best choice."

THE CULTURE CLASH WITHIN

It wasn't just whole-language zealots and California bureaucrats who thought of Open Court as one more traditional phonics program. So did a lot of its own customers and its salespeople. The cultures clashed within the Open Court circle as well as outside it.

"The phonics and letter-perfect writing exercises tend to dominate the program's image among those who choose not to use it," reported Marilyn Jager Adams, author of the definitive 1990 book *Beginning to Read: Thinking and Learning about Print* and later lead author of Open Court's *Collections for Young Scholars*. Even among those who did use *OCRW*, in 1990 she found a disturbing focus on its most traditional aspects. One teacher even set a timer for each activity segment. "Her attention was so riveted on pace and progress through the activities that she appeared not to notice children who were lost or disengaged." Another teacher gave students a ten-word weekly spelling list – a ritualistic focus on an isolated skill that was alien to both Open Court and whole language.

For these paying customers, Open Court as written wasn't traditional enough! Others felt pressure from the accountability movement. The emphasis on testing low-level skills often made it difficult to get teachers to use Open Court properly or even to use it at all (as with math in Florida in 1984). At an October 1983 sales meeting, Karen King reported that Open Court teachers – again, those "within the fold" compared to most educators – were complaining because the company had advised them not to grade some parts of the learning process. They knew the company's long-standing principle of instant feedback, whereby the teacher quickly sees which students are "getting it" and can take remedial action early without ever opening the gradebook. But, according to meeting notes, "They need something concrete to show to parents to verify a grade. They question why there are not more tests. Math is OK but Headway needs more testing on a weekly basis. . . . In West Virginia the teachers make up their own tests."

The irony was vast. Open Court had already almost fallen victim to the false dichotomy between traditionalist "skills" and progressivist "meaning" during California's 1988 reading adoption. Now it was caught again between two political-educational movements – the whole-language movement with roots in progressivism, and the accountability movement with roots in traditionalism.

The University of Illinois' Steve Stahl also observed Open Court classrooms and suggested that at least some of these problems were rooted in the textbooks themselves. *Open Court Reading and Writing,* he said, gave teachers "a highly structured decoding program and vague directions for reading what little text there is," leading teachers to emphasize isolated decoding practice rather than reading for meaning. While *OCRW* tried to emphasize both, "in reality, the program is heavily weighted toward decoding activities of isolated words, with less practice in applying these decoding skills in connected text than is desired." Nor did *OCRW* give the teachers enough help, in his view. "The program is highly explicit about how to teach letter-sound correspondences, yet is very vague in how to handle reading of connected text. . . . For example, in *A Shiny Golden Path,* Lesson 2, although you introduce a major strategy, that of summing up, I get very little sense of how exactly the teacher is supposed to model it for the children."

In other words, Open Court's textbooks as published sometimes failed to carry out its educational vision, and this made it harder to deal with cultural pressures both internal and external. Implementing a vision is hard enough under ideal circumstances. Such circumstances did not prevail at Open Court, partly for management reasons and partly because of the company's chronic shortage of capital.

In the early 1980s, Joe Rubinstein identified one general symptom: a company atmosphere "that does not allow us to profit from our mistakes (as well as from our successes). We seem always to be in a rush; we never take the time to analyze our results."

The rush only intensified in the 1990s, as money and then time began running out. "There was never time to sit back and think," recalls André. One crisis piled on another. The writing and production of the new reading series fell so far behind schedule that newcomers sometimes found themselves drafted into a frenetic process of which they understood little.

"I knew nothing about the program and had never heard terms like phonemic awareness," recalls Beth Niejwik, who was hired as André's assistant in the early 1990s. "Nobody had time to explain anything to me either, so I just found myself sitting in front of a computer in the conference room with the assignment to write five lessons. It is not an exaggeration to say that I had no idea what I was doing." The authors' painstaking philosophical design had to pass through this implementation.

COLLECTIONS FOR YOUNG SCHOLARS

The company's new language arts series, *Collections for Young Scholars,* did more than just reverse the late-'80s move toward the middle, something Carl Bereiter had sought from the beginning. It also attempted to respond to Adams's and Stahl's critiques of *OCRW* and do a better job of bringing the best of both educational traditionalism and progressivism to the classroom. "Teachers and supervisors should know, even as they execute a 'thumb test,' that they are looking at something different," wrote Bereiter in 1990. "The materials should look different in a way that suggests there is something important at hand. We cannot expect that all or even most educators will be sufficiently roused to enquire what is at hand, but some will. . . . For the unaroused majority, it is sufficient that they not be repelled or terrified, that they not put up too much resistance to the enthusiasts in their midst who may see the Open Court materials as offering an exciting opportunity."

Insofar as consistent with Open Court traditions, the first-grade learning-to-read portion of *Collections for Young Scholars* leaned a bit in the direction of whole language. It reflected author Marilyn Adams's view that students need "*both* systematic instruction in phonics *and* rich experience with authentic literature." As she told *Language Arts* magazine in a 1991 interview, "Some of the most productive ways for inducing children to develop interest in, explore, and solidify their knowledge of how the alphabetic system works are activities typically associated with whole language: language-experience activities, booksharing, writing, and the reading of engaging, informative texts. Looking at it this way renders the whole debate more or less moot."

As the students moved into reading-to-learn, Bereiter aimed to provide students with an exciting opportunity to learn, as opposed to a succession of teacher-directed tasks. In commenting on a prototype lesson involving third-graders' browsing before reading, he insisted that this strategy not be practiced to excess and that its purpose be kept in mind.

"They should be able to browse the story on their own and come up with features that puzzle them or catch their attention. Keep in mind that what we ask students to do should bear at least some resemblance to what mature readers do. We do not sit and puzzle long and hard about what a title might indicate (unless perchance the book is sealed in plastic so that we can't look inside it). Neither do we devote intentional effort to prediction [another strategy used by experienced readers]. Predictions sometimes occur as we read, and children should be encouraged to express them when they occur, as in reciprocal teaching. But making a task of it seems to subvert intelligent reading."

Collections for Young Scholars represented the first time since the late 1960s that Open Court's bread-and-butter program had been fundamentally rethought. Most importantly, it incorporated the realization that students have to learn that spoken words and sentences are composed of identifiable and separable sounds ("phonemic awareness"). This is particularly crucial for those children not exposed to songs, jingles, rhymes, chants, and other kinds of language play in their preschool years. Open Court's previous programs had sometimes made an unwarranted assumption about students' abilities by omitting to teach this. (This was one nugget of truth contained in teachers' frequent complaints that Open Court was too hard.) A child who couldn't discern the difference between "f" and "i" in "file" could hardly benefit from associating the sounds with their print symbols.

Blouke and Marianne had made another over-optimistic assumption back in the 1960s, when they thought that it would be enough to expose young readers to literary classics of various cultures. It was not enough, because, as Carl Bereiter pointed out, elite culture had in the past *assumed* that its students already knew how to think for themselves. Now that students came from all kinds of backgrounds, no such assumption could be made. To achieve Open Court's primary goal new ways of teaching had to be found.

TEACHING FROM A TO C

There are three ideal types of teachers, argued Bereiter and Scardamalia in a 1987 article, "An Attainable Version of High Literacy," published in *Curriculum Inquiry*: conventional (teacher A), reformed (teacher B), and intentional-learning (teacher C).

"Teacher A typically assigns reading selections with little preparation and then has students answer oral or workbook questions about them. Teacher A then goes through the selection with the class, asking more questions and explaining what it says for the benefit of those who have not understood it. . . .

"Teacher B is careful to select and sequence reading material so it builds gradually on students' existing knowledge. Before students read a selection, Teacher B carries out activities designed to activate relevant knowledge that students already have available. This might be done by class discussion of the topic, by having students write a story on the topic, or by having students making predictions about the selection to be read. Unfamiliar concepts and terms appearing in the selection are pretaught. Students may be alerted to special points to be on watch for, questions to seek answers for, or difficulties to be prepared for. After the selection has been read, Teacher B guides discussion with questions that lead students to draw inferences from what they have read and to relate what they have read to their other knowledge. . . .

"Teacher C's approach can best be described as taking all the things that Teacher B does and trying to teach students to do them for themselves. This is not accomplished all at once, of course; and so much of Teacher C's behavior resembles that of Teacher B. But Teacher C's goal is that eventually it should not be necessary to conduct activities for activating students' prior knowledge, to ask them questions in order to relate new knowledge to old, and so on. Students should be doing that by themselves and on their own initiative. Teacher C asks students themselves to recognize what is new and what is old information. Instead of asking questions of the students, Teacher C models the process of asking questions of the text or of oneself, and coaches the students in carrying out the modeled process."

Teacher A, Bereiter and Scardamalia suggest, represents what actually goes on in most classrooms. Teacher B represents what most educators think should be going on. Teacher C represents what Open Court thought should be going on.

High literacy and high culture, in this view, don't necessarily have anything to do with grand opera or James Joyce – they have to do with being able to enter into the world of ideas and work within it comfortably. Teacher C's approach is the way to high literacy, defined as literacy that goes beyond responding to immediate situations. "Most learning in school and out in the world results from efforts to deal with conditions, demands, and constraints in the environment and to achieve personal goals within those circumstances. In this sense one may say that the Inuit are adapted to an Arctic environment by virtue of learning. . . . In the same sense, one may say that the typical child achieves literacy by adapting to social expectations and to the school requirements of performing word recognition exercises, reading aloud, answering teacher questions, and the like. The child, in short, does not have to *try* to learn to read but merely has to try to deal with day-to-day situations and school assignments as they appear, and if these are successfully negotiated literacy will automatically ensue. But the literacy that ensues is the literacy sustained and required by the surrounding environment; and this, we are saying, is low literacy."

In practice, it's easy to miss the distinction between Teachers B and C. *CYS* author Valerie Anderson could spot it a mile off, though. A draft *CYS* teacher's guide suggested to the teacher in the course of a selection about baby animals, "You may wish to wonder aloud about a few things as you read, and encourage the children to do the same. For example, you might say, 'I wonder what other baby animals look like their parents.' Invite the children to respond to such wonderings. If necessary, prompt them with appropriate questions (for example: 'Can you think of other baby animals that look like their parents? What about pets?')."

That final piece of advice sounds innocuous enough, but it did not please Anderson. "DO NOT EVER PROMPT WITH QUESTIONS. CUT CUT CUT," she wrote. "If they cannot think of anything, offer an example, e.g., I know that little alligators look just like tiny grown up alligators. Also, [prompting with questions] shifts the attention to answering the teachers' questions rather than focusing on the wondering itself. I urge you pleasantly not to do this."

RECIPROCAL TEACHING

Clearly, being Teacher C – to be able to model "wondering" without doing the children's wondering for them – isn't easy. In their article "Communities of Learning and Thinking," Ann Brown and Joseph Campione describe one way of doing it, called "reciprocal teaching," which also incorporated some notions congenial to whole-language advocates. Brown was an author of *Open Court Reading and Writing,* but her ideas seem to have been more fully embodied in its successor program.

In reciprocal teaching, an adult teacher and a group of students take turns "being the teacher," i.e., leading a discussion about material that they have either read or listened to. The learning leader uses questions and summaries to begin and end discussion, and, in between, "attempts to *clarify* that any comprehension problems that might arise occur opportunistically when someone misunderstands, or does not know the meaning of a concept, word, or phrase, etc. And, finally, the leader asks for *predictions* about future content if this is appropriate. The *cooperative* nature of the procedure is an essential feature," with all members of the group taking turns being learning leaders.

If reciprocal teaching works right, everyone is trying to learn (or comprehend, or "construct meaning"), not trying to find the right answer that the teacher already has. In other words, the students take on the cognitive work the teacher would have done for them if the teacher had been the only one questioning, summarizing, clarifying, and predicting. It contrasts sharply with conventional "reading groups," in which teachers of the A or B variety assign the text and "dole reading out in small pieces, and students have no right to put the task aside," and in which "students read in order to prove to the teacher that they have read; to answer questions posed by the teacher, who, clearly, already knows the answer."

Learning through reciprocal teaching, when it occurs, is both more fun and more lasting. It also asks more of the teacher, as Lawrence Cremin observed long ago that serious progressive education would. Could most teachers handle it? Bereiter thought so, but not without help.

"Building a literate community in the classroom," he suggested to his fellow authors and company personnel, was the primary goal of *CYS,* and it did not presume exceptional skills. "We must be careful to design the program so that teachers new to this approach can feel comfortable with it and experience success at the same time that they are growing into the new role. To prevent backsliding toward conventional teaching we need to provide (1) strong reminders of the ultimate goal and (2) activity structures that result in natural pressures toward teacher development."

Accordingly *CYS* organized its readings, artwork, writing, and discussion around "explorable concepts" – in the first two readers, "games," "folk tales," "keep trying," "being afraid," and "homes." These were not supposed to be simply a way of grouping selections. Each reading selection under a given concept would ideally either expand the students' understanding of a familiar concept, or flesh out a powerful new one. The concept units became the program's center, around which all reading, writing, discussion, and research was to be conducted. They were to make possible the cumulative learning that starts and feeds any learning community.

COMMUNITIES OF LEARNING, OR MORE ACTIVITIES?

As the new selections for *Collections for Young Scholars* passed over his desk, Blouke found himself increasingly pleased. "Not only are the explorable concepts everything the authors wanted, but in my own judgment they are closer to my original idea for the readers than anything Open Court has published in the past twenty years."

The new program was of course subject to multicultural requirements, but Bereiter followed another Open Court tradition when he emphasized universal principles over surface diversity. "In one story currently under consideration," he wrote in 1991, "a little boy in Puerto Rico is trying to raise money to buy a gift for his mother. There is a lot of local color which, if treated as the main ingredient, would turn the piece into a travelogue. I can imagine a real time-waster of a lesson that has the kids looking at tourist views of Puerto Rico or discussing exotic places they have visited. The boy's problem, however, is not just how to get money but how to get it by honorable means. He is intent on giving good value for money and will not take more than he thinks he has earned. This is a theme of universal significance, well worth developing."

CYS did not succeed in solving the perennial teachers' guide headache – that may have been too much to hope for in view of its other innovations. In the field, Karen Hansill found that, if anything, it was harder to teach from the published teachers' guides than *OCRW* had been. The program was still not self-explanatory. "There were too many pieces," she recalls. "Each lesson had three parts, but you were supposed to do some of each part each day. It was hard to figure out how to pace things. It was a good program, but a heavy burden for training."

Like its predecessors, *CYS* depended on a devoted and knowledgeable force of salespeople and consultants to interpret it. Comprehension activities were not labeled in *CYS* as they had been in *OCRW,* and sure enough, a company field note from early 1995 reports, "Some of our more traditional teachers are unsure of how to identify comprehension instruction."

Would the education culture encapsulate and neutralize *CYS* too? "The cultural shift that is implied in the new cognitive approaches remains poorly understood in the educational community," Bereiter wrote early in 1997 – "the shift, that is, from classroom life organized around activities to classroom life organized around the pursuit of knowledge. Instead, reciprocal teaching, communities of learners, and other transformations of classroom culture are merely perceived as new activities to replace or supplement old ones."

Ann Brown agreed. "Too often something called reciprocal teaching is practiced in such a way that the principles of learning it was meant to foster are lost, or at best relegated to a minor position. The surface rituals of questioning, summarizing, and so forth are engaged in, divorced from the goal of reading for understanding that they were designed to serve."

What Open Court asked of educators was not just novel and time-consuming. It was *hard.* Said Brown, "It is easier to organize drill and practice in decontextualized skills to mastery, or to manage 164 behavioral objectives, than it is to create and sustain environments that foster thought, thought about powerful ideas. We are asking a great deal from everyone in the learning community."

Conclusion

"Inertia will always lead the schools to try to assimilate the new knowledge to their old, established practices . . . only continued vigilance, continued testing and criticism, can hope to make headway against the overwhelming current." – Blouke Carus, September 24, 1985

THE COMPANY

ONE CHAPTER IN the Sisyphean struggle to change the education culture ended in March 1996. After Open Court's bankers delivered a financial ultimatum, the company's textbook operations were sold to SRA/McGraw-Hill. Sales of the textbooks have more than doubled since then, fueling Blouke's optimism about the future of American education.

This book is already long enough without taking up this sequel. Open Court's experience between 1962 and 1996 already shows that no single change can alter the culture of American public education. If the ingrained expectations of parents, students, administrators, and teachers remain largely the same, even the best educational tools can go unused or misused.

Open Court's experience also shows that a business-reform hybrid has advantages over government-funded programs or non-profit advocacy groups, the usual vehicles for reform. The company was born at about the same time as the post-Sputnik curriculum-reform groups. These groups focused almost exclusively on creating better textbooks, but failed to get them into the schools. As a business and not a government program, Open Court had to do both. It could not have survived if it had maintained its original plan of changing American education by just offering a better textbook. It had to learn that better books would not sell themselves, and that the books themselves had to be better in unexpected ways. Simply exposing students and teachers to high culture would not work in the late twentieth century.

As a business-reform hybrid, Open Court thus had to respond to the market – and in doing so, it also had to be more balanced than advocacy groups that rally volunteers. Political scientist Jane Mansbridge has written, "Mobilizing volunteers often requires an exaggerated, black or white vision of events to justify spending time and money on the cause." Open Court had to present itself less stridently, because many of its potential adversaries were also its potential customers.

While responding to the market gave the company an edge on the ivory tower and the lobbyists, it also exacted a toll. Open Court reflected within itself the same tension between change and the status quo that existed in the outside world. Authors and executives with their eyes on the prize took a different view from those dealing with customers who repeatedly asked for something familiar. Both viewpoints have validity and need to remain in tension – a challenge to tax a virtuoso manager, something Open Court never had.

But no amount of effort or increased sophistication enabled the company to move beyond phonics, which Blouke always saw as a side issue. Customers and opponents alike focused on how to teach beginning reading. Some even characterized Open Court as a "traditional" program because of its initial phonics approach. Company leadership wasn't able to direct attention to the basic issue that had inspired Blouke to publish textbooks in the first place – how to teach all children, not just to read, but to read, write, speak, and listen critically.

Nor could the company keep from being whipsawed between the two educational traditions it sought to blend. Progressive-minded educators scorned Open Court's traditionalist elements like intensive phonics and direct teaching. Traditionalists and plodders didn't understand Open Court's progressive and flexible elements like Workshop.

THE CULTURE

Over the last half-century, the education culture too has had to change. In the heyday of "life-adjustment" schooling fifty years ago, we were told that not all children needed to learn to read and write. Now lip service is paid to the goal of everyone learning. Whole language is a more appealing fad than look-say. The 1980s California textbook adoption charade paid tribute to reform goals while largely blocking their achievement, a different approach from the 1950s style of slamming the door.

But the culture has not had to change much. Its most subtle method of self-perpetuation remains its ability to transmute gold into lead: objectives into activities, skills into subject-matter, cognitive strategies into lists of rules to memorize. Thus Open Court found that teachers demanded books that included comprehension questions after each reading selection – in the implicit belief that assigning students to answer those questions was the same thing as showing students how to extract meaning from each selection on their own. The culture can assume a veneer of progressivism or traditionalism as the times dictate, but its routines lie deeper than ideology.

The education culture's anti-intellectual effects on the schools continue. "In the closing years of the century," Diane Ravitch writes in *Left Back*, "it was obvious that the quality of schooling had not kept pace with its quantity. Students were staying in school longer than ever, but were they learning more than ever? Few thought so, nor did available evidence suggest that they were. More students were going on to college than ever before, but nearly a third of them found it necessary to take remedial courses in reading, writing, or mathematics."

This fundamental problem will not be addressed without fundamental change. But the keepers of the culture continue to defend the status quo by attacking efforts to put rigorous educational research to work in the classroom. And their anti-intellectual message continues to be celebrated in the media. On January 9, 2002, the day President Bush signed the bipartisan Elementary and Secondary Education Act ("No Child Left Behind") that emphasized research-based teaching methods, the *New York Times* published a background piece in which reporter Diana Jean Schemo devoted more space to those complaining about the research underlying the bill than to those explaining and defending it.

Schemo first quoted Assistant Secretary of Education Susan B. Neuman, who said, "I want to change the face of reading instruction across the United States, from an art to a science." The touchstone for Neuman's proposed change, the 2000 National Reading Panel report (NRP), highlighted research demonstrating the value of systematic phonics instruction. Then Schemo quoted three different sources who criticized it: Alan Farstrup of the International Reading Association, Jerry Sroufe of the American Educational Research Association, and Elaine Garan of California State University, Fresno, writing in the *Phi Delta Kappan.* They favored what Schemo described as "qualitative" research supporting whole language. (The term "qualitative" was left undefined and unchallenged.) Garan was given space to expound on how the thirty-eight studies that met the NRP's criteria for rigor focused on "isolated skills" as opposed to "authentic application." Neuman was given a weak one-sentence reply and Sroufe got the last word, implying once again that the NRP's selection of studies constituted a self-fulfilling prophecy.

The story employed a double standard: research supporting systematic phonics (or any systematic plan of instruction, for that matter) was held to a high standard of proof, while whole language was said to be supported by "qualitative" research – i.e., observations that are non-quantitative, small-scale, and difficult or impossible to reproduce. The double standard was deployed in an effort to keep rigorous research at bay and maintain the status quo in classrooms.

Coverage elsewhere added outright misrepresentation to a similar bias. Writing in the *Nation* magazine on January 28, Stephen Metcalf described phonics as "traditional and rote," apparently unaware that the very program at issue (Open Court's) had been giving teachers the tools to teach phonics in creative, non-traditional ways for more than thirty-five years. Metcalf quoted Gerald Coles, author of *Reading Lessons: The Debate over Literacy,* who described phonics as "a way of thinking about illiteracy that doesn't involve thinking about larger social injus-

tices." In fact, phonics advocates including Rudolf Flesch and
Blouke Carus had long considered phonics a way of thinking
about illiteracy that could help remedy a fundamental social
injustice. Time and again over the past four decades, they pointed out that when schools deny students the best possible beginning-reading instruction, the students must depend on compensation from literate parents. The children of less-educated parents don't have this at-home compensation; hence they often
become poor readers and are relegated to low places in the social-
economic hierarchy.

It might be possible to construct an argument that Flesch and
Carus and others were mistaken in thinking that systematic phonics is the best possible form of beginning-reading instruction. But
to say that they had no interest in thinking about large social
injustices is not an argument. It's merely a lie, one that serves to
keep the status quo in place in most classrooms.

Even in places where one might expect more careful thinking, we find outright rejection of the idea that education could
become more scientific than artistic. In 2002, Great Books
Foundation president Peter Temes published a book with the
straightforward title *Against School Reform (And in Praise of Great
Teaching)*. The book makes a number of strong points against
purely institutional school reforms and in favor of a more
demanding career ladder for teachers. But Temes denies the
validity of educational research of any kind (because in actual
classrooms all variables can't be held constant). And he contends
that teaching should involve nothing but continuous experimen-
tation. "The biology teacher who solves the big problem of how to
teach cell division – not just today but for years to come, forever,
by writing a lesson plan that will cover the bases without fail –
misses the opportunity to see the problem as a new, small-scale
challenge every time a class approaches it. . . . The very best teachers seldom rely on tried-and-true lessons. They understand the
seductive power of the experiment."

This approach goes well beyond the reminder that teachers
should always keep learning and improving. If taken seriously, it
seems intellectually perverse. Would we encourage doctors to

regard every patient as a fresh chance to try untested new thera-
pies? To his credit, Temes can't maintain his stance, and at one
point criticizes his alma mater, New York City's John Dewey High
School, because "it failed to move beyond the culture of experiment and study how and why things at the school worked the way
they did. The idea that the experiment could be assessed and
improved year by year was entirely absent." But Temes has already
denied that research can provide a yardstick for such attempts at
assessment and improvement. So glorifying the gifted few who
can improvise brilliantly every time serves to – surprise! – keep the
status quo in place in most classrooms.

As these examples show, the education culture is alive, influential, and presenting itself more smoothly than fifty years ago.
Decades of educational failure and sophisticated ridicule have
not broken the culture's grip on American schooling. The lessons
Open Court learned while confronting it in the marketplace in
the 1960s, 1970s, 1980s, and 1990s remain all too relevant.

THE END

Do children still learn from "spelling lists"? Do they walk through
science "projects" judged by slightly older students? Are teachers
told that all learning is natural and that direct teaching is unnecessary or undesirable? Is math still seen as a set of procedures
rather than a universe of ideas? Do schools refuse to purchase
textbooks unless they have comprehension questions printed
after each selection? Do they resist research and accountability?
Are teachers denied the paid time to get together to develop and
teach and critique model lessons?

When we can answer "No" to these and similar questions,
then American education will have begun to fulfill the promise
that Open Court represented – real education for all.

Index